I0605586

Praise for
It's All Within You

"Having seen Millana float and flow gracefully between healing circles and social circles, I can say (with confidence) that she embodies the spirit of someone who genuinely wants to bring love, light, and deeper connection to the world, and I'm happy she has collected all her learnings, insights, and downloads into this book; let's continue to read, learn about ourselves and each other, and raise the vibration!"

—**Tino DeMartino,** head of wellness for Soho House North America

"In a world that tells us to look everywhere else for healing, Millana Snow's *It's All Within You* reminds us of the revolutionary truth: You already have everything you need. This book is a road map back to your authentic Self—written by someone who has walked the path. Snow's seven principles will help you stop searching outside yourself and guide you home."

—**Noor Tagouri,** journalist, activist, motivational speaker, and producer of *The Trouble They've Seen* docuseries

"I've had the privilege of witnessing Millana's incredible journey and watching her grow into a powerful force for healing and transformation. In *It's All Within You*, she invites readers to stop seeking solutions outside themselves and embrace the truth that real, lasting healing comes from within. Her message couldn't be timelier or more needed, offering a heartfelt and deeply embodied guide for anyone ready to reclaim their wholeness."

—**Len Burnett,** founder of VIBE and *UPTOWN* Magazine

"There are a lot of people doing this work now, but Millana is the real deal. She's been holding it down in the wellness space for over ten years. This book distills so much of what makes her work powerful. *It's All Within You* will guide you back home to yourself. If you're feeling stuck or disconnected, let this book remind you that you have even more power than you imagine."

—**Justin Michael Williams,** author of *Stay Woke*

"Since 2013, Millana and I have walked parallel paths in this ever-evolving world of wellness. She's always been ahead of the curve—bold, rooted, and unafraid to tell the truth. *It's All Within You* isn't just timely—it's timeless."

—**Sah D'Simone,** trauma-informed spiritual teacher and global humanitarian

"I've seen Millana change lives with this work—including her own. As an Olympic athlete, I know what true dedication looks like, and she has it. Her consistency, depth, and integrity are rare. If she's guiding you, trust that you're in powerful hands."

—**Louise Hazel,** Olympian and founder of SLAY

"From my first sixty seconds with Miss Millana, I knew she was the real deal. Her work isn't about performance or perfection but about returning to the part of yourself that remembers how to feel safe and clear. We dwell in a world that constantly pulls us outward into distraction and capitalism—even the wellness industry isn't exempt!—so an invitation inward is more important than ever. Millana is a relatable yet potent reminder that healing is accessible to us all. Our breath is not solely a machine humming in the background of our lives but a nervous system MVP that we can intentionally use anytime, anywhere, free of charge, and free of fine print. Millana shows us that breathwork isn't a luxury—it's a lifeline."

—**Tracy G,** on-air radio host of *Sway in the Morning*

"Working with Millana has been one of the most transformative experiences of my life—both personally and creatively. I truly believe anyone who feels stuck—whether creatively, emotionally, or spiritually—needs to read Millana's book and experience her work. She has a unique gift to help people see themselves fully and will guide them through deep transformation."

—**Regulo Caro,** celebrated Mexican singer and songwriter

"I had a transformative experience with Millana; I found myself traveling across the country to see my ailing mother in a highly emotional encounter that had tears streaming down my face. Millana unlocked a door inside me, and I am so grateful that I was able to walk through it."

—**Nelson George,** American author, National Book Critics Circle Award nominee, music and culture critic, columnist, journalist, and filmmaker

Working with Millana has been one of the most transformative experiences of my life, both personally and creatively. I came to her at a time when I felt completely blocked—emotionally, spiritually, and artistically. Through her guidance and self-healing work, Millana helped me unlock my sacral energy, which was deeply blocked by past traumas I didn't even realize were still affecting me.

This process allowed me to heal emotional wounds that had been limiting my ability to fully express who I am—not only as an artist but also as a person. Since then, I've felt a level of creative freedom, clarity, and confidence that I hadn't experienced in years. It's like she helped me reconnect to the purest version of myself.

I truly believe anyone who feels stuck—whether creatively, emotionally, or spiritually—needs to read Millana's book and experience her work. She has a unique gift to help you see yourself fully and guide you through deep transformation.

—**Regulo Caro,** celebrated Mexican singer and songwriter

It's All Within You

It's All Within You

7 Principles to Access Your Innate Power and Heal from the Inside Out

MILLANA SNOW

New York Boston

The tools and information presented herein are not intended to replace the services of trained health professionals or be a substitute for medical advice. You are advised to consult with your health care professional with regard to matters relating to your health, and in particular regarding matters that may require diagnosis or medical attention.

Details relating to the author's life are reflected faithfully to the best of their ability, while recognizing that others who were present might recalls things differently. Names and identifying details have been changed to protect the privacy and safety of others, including clients who shared their stories for this book.

Cover Design by Dean Grenier

Balance
Hachette Book Group
1290 Avenue of the Americas
New York, NY 10104
GCP-Balance.com
@GCPBalance

First Edition: November 2025

Balance is an imprint of Grand Central Publishing. The Balance name and logo are registered trademarks of Hachette Book Group, Inc.

Print book interior design by Amy Quinn

Library of Congress Cataloging-in-Publication Data

Name: Snow, Millana author.
Title: It's all within you: 7 principles to access your innate power and heal from the inside out / Millana Snow.
Description: First edition. | New York: Balance, 2025. | Includes bibliographical references and index.
Identifiers: LCCN 2025019767 | ISBN 9781538772645 hardcover | ISBN 9781538772652 paperback | ISBN 9781538772669 ebook
Subjects: LCSH: Self-actualization (Psychology) | Mind and body.
Classification: LCC BF637.S4 .S653 2025
LC record available at https://lccn.loc.gov/2025019767

ISBNs: 978-1-538-77264-5 (hardcover); 978-1-538-77266-9 (ebook)

Printed in the United States of America

LSC-C

Printing 1, 2025

Contents

Author's Note

Names and details have been changed to protect the identity of those mentioned.

It's All Within You

Introduction

He pulled me into the bathroom in the back of the house on the outskirts of Denver, Colorado. The pitch-black darkness inside the room transported me to another realm. A nasty place I could only leave if he let me. He threatened to beat me with a belt, but suffocated me instead.

I never knew what I'd done, but I knew it must have been something bad. My breath was taken away as punishment. It started when I was only five years old. He would cover my mouth and nose with just one hand. I don't remember being afraid so much as hating the feeling that I couldn't escape. It made me hate the dark. It was only when it was pitch black that I was forced to hang on like that. I was hanging on the edge, hoping my breath would return. Oh, the tightness in my chest. The help I couldn't get. The scream I couldn't let out. The breath I couldn't let go of or take in. I was just hanging on, waiting for it to be over.

Nearly thirty years later, I returned to that room in a self-guided Integrative Breathwork practice. I saw my younger self through the darkness. But this time, I was in the corner, shining a light that only I could see but that my younger self could feel. He was suffocating me, but I was there as an adult now, willing young Millana to continue on. Through my conscious breath, I entered deep time. I traveled to a realm where my memory was made real again. Time and space flattened until I was the little girl, the woman remembering her, and the Soul who knew it was passing through. I didn't know it when I was a kid, but it was because I was suffocated that I would find a way to reclaim my breath a million times over. I would transform this trauma into the calling that has helped millions of others reclaim their breath, too. My whole life would become a living testament to how precious the breath is.

Reclaiming my breath through breathwork became a turning point, a doorway back to my higher Self. But my journey of healing was a long and winding road. Each chapter of my life revealed the insights that eventually became the foundation for the seven principles shared in this book. And yet, these principles supported me long before I consciously recognized them.

Presence emerged from my loneliest days as a latchkey kid. By thirteen, after moving eleven times and attending seven different schools, I learned the power of being present, even in the midst of constant upheaval. I found stillness in meditation, chanting, and energy healing, practices my grandmother taught me when I was just four years old.

Love was something I deeply yearned for and struggled with, but my early spiritual practices opened pathways to self-love and compassion. Even through abuse at home and bullying at school, I learned that the love I most needed was the love I could offer myself.

Integration was seeded in my early experiences with the unseen world. As a child, I lived fully in my gifts, but to survive as I got older, I hid the brightest parts of myself behind a carefully crafted mask of "normal" to fit in wherever we moved.

Grief revealed itself through the loneliness of my childhood. The constant endings and beginnings taught me that loss could become fuel for transformation, and that longing could be fertile soil for new beginnings.

Faith became clear when I moved to New York City at nineteen with only my dreams and determination, without any family support. I was a wild child living on school loans, and in three years, I had my dream job at *Vibe* magazine, graduated with honors, and won *Project Runway*—all through a process that can make your inner visions an outer reality.

Joy surfaced when I finally started living what felt true to me. Soon after *Project Runway*, I hosted an online travel series in China that later won a Webby award. Out of my passion for healing, I launched rooftop yoga and meditation experiences in New York, London, and Los Angeles. Once I prioritized my personal values in my everyday life, I had more joy—and the opportunities, money, and recognition came to me with ease.

Rest became essential when I left New York for Los Angeles so I could live closer to nature and create more space in my life. In LA, my first business failed and I was forced to rest and reflect on how I needed to grow. After time, I started my current community from the ground up as a way of life, not just a business. After years of success with thousands of one-on-one and group healing sessions, I eventually began training hundreds of breathwork teachers.

I have been a seeker and a healer since I was a child, but my life has more often been messy than put together—burnout, toxic relationships, dreams that seemed to run me into the ground instead of lifting me up.

Does any of that sound familiar? Did you grow up as the new kid over and over because life kept you moving? Or maybe you hid the brightest parts of yourself so no one would think you were "too much." Perhaps you still hold your breath in meetings the way you once did in childhood, or hit career highs yet collapse into exhaustion behind closed doors. Do you promise yourself you will finally rest and then chase the next achievement anyway?

I know what it's like to have these oh-so-human experiences. And I finally know what it's like to be free of what I thought I would have to carry. So have the thousands of people who have come through my courses, sessions, and trainings. The seven principles you are about to learn carried us to the other side of those patterns, and they can carry you there too.

Over time, I created frameworks to keep what worked and shed what didn't, gathered research to see what science and ancient traditions have found, and shared the practices and principles that I learned with thousands of people all over the world to see what worked for them. After over a decade of pulling my personal and professional findings together, I realized I had insights that others could benefit from learning. I'm offering them to you here.

Working with these principles is meant to help you tap into the power that already lives inside you. Nothing about you needs fixing. Healing is remembering who you've always been but couldn't reach—the version of you that the world and past trauma made you forget. The healing we'll do together is about turning past hurt into the very purpose and freedom you came here for. One self-guided breathwork session alone can impact your life in a profound way.

We are living at a pace nobody was built for. The news never sleeps: Wars scroll across every screen, storms and fires redraw entire coastlines, and whole communities wonder where their next meal will come from. Violence, hunger, and displacement feel closer each day, even when they erupt oceans away. Deadlines still demand attention, notifications still ping before dawn, and somehow we are supposed to keep going.

If your nervous system registers that weight, if your gut or your sleepless nights insist something must change, this book meets you at the right moment—because the change begins inside you. And when you shift, healing ripples out farther than the eye can see. In times like these, we need to get back to the basics of what heals and restores us rather than what causes more harm.

While this book is practical, it is also an experience that can shift things and surface trauma that you didn't even realize was there. Take your time and move at your own pace. And when you're reminded to breathe, take each opportunity to settle into how you feel.

The journey ahead moves in two clear stages:

Part 1 weaves story with the neuroscience of breathwork so you understand how a single session can flip your nervous system from panic to deep presence.

Part 2 devotes one full chapter to each principle—Presence, Love, Integration, Grief, Faith, Joy, Rest—pairing real-life cases with step-by-step practices and guided breathwork.

Make space for what resonates by trying the "How to Practice This Principle" exercises at the end of each chapter. And remember, this isn't a manual intended to fix you, but a reminder of the power already inside you. Everything you seek is within you.

So let's dive in. But first, let's take a deep breath.

It's All Within You

PART 1

It's All Within You

CHAPTER 1

The Four Tenets

CLOSE YOUR EYES AND IMAGINE WALKING INTO A BEAUTIFUL home. As soon as you step through the front door, every problem, burden, trauma, or worry you ever had is left outside. And as you walk around the most gorgeous space you have ever seen, you start to realize that this is the home you have always dreamed of.

For the first time in a long time, you feel safe, joyful, and like you are just where you belong. Your breath settles and every layer of you relaxes at once: Your jaw unclenches, the lower back releases, thoughts untangle, and compassion floods in. Spending even just a few minutes here is like getting a year of the best sleep all at once. But you're not asleep, you're fully conscious.

This isn't a dream. It's your inner world when you are truly at peace. And it's a place that you have access to through the altered states that arise in a breathwork session. This inner sanctuary, where body, mind, heart, and spirit are at rest, is the home you have searched for all along.

Take a moment to imagine being there. Breathe and feel into this place inside of yourself. Close your eyes and take two long inhales through the mouth. Take the first breath down to your belly so it balloons out, the second into your chest. Pause before you slowly exhale. If you tune in, you can sense what's there in the pause between breaths.

Sometimes it's hard to experience your inner world as some heavenly realm because parts of you are scared, neglected, and angry. Some rooms are still locked: anger pushed into closets, grief tucked under floorboards. Before you can feel at home, you need to tend to what you've been resisting.

But here's the good news: Those painful parts of you that seem so stressed or scared just need your love and attention. Rest assured, we will do that together, and it will be so worth it. Because when your inner world is thriving, you stop searching for things outside yourself. Because you find everything you need within.

Are you ready to feel at home again? Here are the four foundational tenets that will help you to tap into your innate power and peace within.

FOUR FOUNDATIONAL TENETS TO GUIDE YOU HOME

1. EXPERIENCE > ANALYSIS

Most of what you've been told about healing is half truth. Healing doesn't come from thinking or even talking about things. Healing happens through experiencing how you feel. Feeling, rather than thinking, is how you heal. While talk therapy sessions and empowerment seminars can bring great insight and understanding, the deeper inner resolution you're seeking happens outside of logic, in the realm of the experiential and the ineffable.

When you gain insights through talk therapy, it's like getting a map. You move forward by thinking your way through things. But while mental analysis can show you which way to go, points of interest, even what others have seen along the way, like a map, it can only get you so far. You still have to go there in your body. *Feeling is how you get there. Experiencing* is how you do the "walking" that takes you off the map in your head and into your embodied healing journey.

Research backs this up. Talking about our feelings can help, but deeper healing often happens when we feel those feelings. A landmark study (Pascual-Leone and Greenberg 2007) found that the people who allowed themselves to fully experience their emotions instead of just analyzing them made the biggest and most lasting changes in therapy.

Neuroscience research shows that emotionally charged moments become lasting memories. Repeated or significant emotional experiences become the foundation for how we view ourselves and the world. For instance, if you regularly felt unsafe or unseen during high-emotion moments, your brain may associate those emotions with ideas like, "I'm not safe" or "I don't matter." These aren't just thoughts; they're embodied beliefs shaped by lived experience.

This is because emotions activate the amygdala, whose primary role is to detect emotional significance, especially when something feels threatening, exciting, or deeply meaningful. This helps the brain focus on and prioritize what's happening in the moment—especially if it seems important for survival or connection. The amygdala is directly connected to the hippocampus, the part of the brain responsible for forming and organizing long-term memories. When the amygdala is highly activated (due to emotional activity), it sends signals to the hippocampus that say, "This experience is important. Don't forget it." That's why we remember where we were during a breakup, a birth, or a moment of awe—but not what we had for lunch three days ago. Over time, these emotionally encoded memories shape how we navigate relationships, safety, and self-worth.

Thankfully our memories and the associations our brains make are malleable. As neuropsychologist Louis Cozolino (2017) puts it, "Neural networks that are activated, fired, and wired together during emotional experiences are more effectively modified during states that recreate those same emotional experiences." In other words: The emotional charge that built the belief is the same key that unlocks it. If a memory is recalled while you're in an emotionally open or altered state (such as feeling safe, loved, or deeply present), your memories can be reconsolidated—that is, rewired—with a new emotional association of safety.

This requires:

- Deep presence and attuned focus to reenter the emotional state in which a memory was formed
- Activation of the emotional memory (feeling it, not just naming it)
- A newly felt emotional experience, insight, or meaning of that memory or embodied belief
- Integration over time, often through repeated experience to reestablish trust in the new association of feelings and beliefs

Pause, and take a breath to feel. What are you feeling right now? Let yourself feel it before you give it a label.

2. EVERYTHING IS FOR YOUR USE

Picture a compost pile: a month's worth of food scraps, today's coffee grounds, even the weeds you pulled weeks ago, all breaking down into soil rich enough to grow an entire garden. That is how we will treat everything life throws at you—in other words, everything can be used and nothing is wasted. Throughout this book, and in all my work, you will hear me say "Everything is for your use." We make everything workable, no matter how mundane or earth-shattering. Whether it's the mundane memory of falling off your bike for the first time, a relationship ending, or hearing a doctor say "terminal," you still hold the choice to make it for your use. Inconvenience can become opportunity, distraction can spark inspiration, and pain can reveal purpose.

Psychologists Richard Tedeschi and Lawrence Calhoun (2004) call this "post-traumatic growth." In their seminal review, they found that up to 70 percent of people who faced major adversity—serious illness, combat, natural disaster—reported at least one positive life change directly linked to the trauma. The gains showed up in five areas: deeper appreciation of life, stronger relationships, new possibilities, personal strength, and spiritual expansion. The key was not the event itself, but how people worked with it: deliberate reflection, sharing the story aloud, and asking what meaning could be made from the wreckage. They took in what was available to them and then composted the scraps.

Rather than labeling a cancer diagnosis a death sentence, this viewpoint asks: How might I feel through what this is trying to offer me? How might it invite you to embrace life more fully? How is this meant to help me heal and grow in ways I never before imagined?

This process comes up in both big and small ways. Even a police siren during meditation can become a reminder that calm is possible amid chaos. Through this lens, everything is grist for the mill. Life conspires for you, not against you. As you work (and play) with the things that challenge you, keep asking yourself, *How is this for my use?* This is a real inquiry, one that inspires an openness to more possibilities rather than spiritual bypassing.

Let's do it right now. Pause and think of one current irritation or hurt. Allow yourself to feel it in your body. Breathe deeply in and out through the nose three times. Now imagine breaking the hurt and anger down into fertile soil. How could this be useful for you right now?

3. WHAT YOU RESIST PERSISTS

Think of life as a flowing river. If you allow yourself to change, you flow with the river downstream. But if you resist the flow of change, the river's current becomes stronger. The more you resist, the stronger the opposing force, and the more energy it takes to hold it back. The river always wins.

When you resist change, you resist an intelligence that far outweighs the ego's. The energy required to continue to resist what needs to be faced in order for you to change eventually leads to a collapse or crisis. The longer you resist, the more dramatic the eventual fallout will be. Resistance is a human reaction. It will come up. This is why it's so important to remember that "everything is for your use"—so that you can stop resisting the change that is already happening. Put simply, acceptance and surrender are key.

This isn't just my theory. Science backs up what ancient wisdom has taught: Resistance tends to strengthen what we're trying to avoid. Studies on Acceptance and Commitment Therapy show that trying to control or push away painful thoughts and emotions usually makes them louder, not quieter (Hayes et al. 2006). A review of sixty-six studies found that people who practiced acceptance rather than resistance saw better outcomes with anxiety, depression, and overall well-being. Psychology researcher Daniel Wegner (1994) called this the "ironic process"—the more you try not to think about something, the more it takes over your mind. As Wegner put it, "The paradoxical effect of thought suppression is that it produces the very preoccupation that it is directed against." In short, acceptance clears the path for change; resistance keeps us stuck.

Resistance is the mind's attempt to control what it doesn't want to accept. But healing begins the moment we stop fighting and start allowing. This isn't about accepting harm or injustice; it's about accepting the truth of what is. When we stop resisting, the experience itself begins to shift. Not because the facts change but because our relationship to them does.

Resistance can come in the form of denial, rejection, neglect, and obstinance. It shows up in many forms of expression—mentally, physically, behaviorally, and emotionally—in relationships as well as in your creative and healing inner work.

Resistance Red Flags

- **Mind:** rigid loops of thought, denial, distraction
- **Body:** chronic pain, restless nights, tension
- **Emotions:** sudden anger, numbness, feeling disconnected
- **Behavior:** withdrawal, codependency, numbing scrolls
- **Spirit/Creativity:** writer's block, endless planning, procrastination, and perfectionism

Notice any of these in your life right now? That's your cue to pause, breathe, and let the current of life flow by being present with it instead of pushing against it.

4. SET AND SETTING MATTER

Imagine you are planting a seed. In neglected soil it struggles to sprout. In rich, well-tended earth it bursts into bloom. Healing work is the same. While you can transcend even the most challenging of circumstances and environments, the right set and setting can make it more enjoyable. It's far easier when you adjust the setting that supports your mind, body, and spirit.

Decades of research confirm that our environment shapes our inner state. Patients in hospital rooms with natural light recover faster and need less pain medication than those kept in dim, windowless wards (Ulrich 1984).

You can create the optimal conditions for your healing to thrive. Choose a time that works for you to play within, and make sure you'll have time afterward to integrate and rest. To the best of your ability, when you're ready, find a private spot where you can cry, scream, laugh, dance, or simply sit—where you can express freely without editing for others. Be sure to have plenty of water on hand. Turn off your phone or set to Do Not Disturb. Wear something loose and comfortable. Soften the light and open a window for fresh air. It is also important that you set intentions before you begin, and make a clear closing when you finish.

In general, prioritize rest, hydration, and nourishing food in your life so that your body can fully show up for whatever emerges.

Now take a breath and set your intention for the healing you would like to unfold in working with this book. What set and setting might you create to support you in that?

Integrative Breathwork

Let's dig into the basics of the most foundational practice of the work that we are doing together: Integrative Breathwork. This is the same practice that I shared in the beginning of the book. Before sharing how to do it or more stories about what I have seen and experienced with it, I'll give you a more scientific breakdown so you can get the full picture of just how powerful this practice is.

Breathwork is the practice of intentionally modulating your breath to change your mind, body, and emotions. Through the conscious control of your breath, you shift out of your body's fight-or-flight response (sympathetic nervous system) and into your body's rest-and-digest state (parasympathetic nervous system) where healing naturally occurs.

Breathwork has a real, noticeable impact on how we feel. A 2023 review (Fincham et al.) looked at hundreds of people across different studies and found that slow, steady breathing helped lower stress, anxiety, and symptoms of depression. A 2023 meta-analysis in *Scientific Reports* found that slow nasal breathing reduced anxiety by approximately 20 percent across eighteen randomized controlled trials (Zaccaro et al. 2023).

Sustaining the Integrative Breathwork's deep breathing pattern can also release endorphins, the natural painkillers that promote a feeling of well-being, while lowering levels of stress chemicals like cortisol and adrenaline. Marathoners speak of a "runner's high"; breathwork taps into the same internal pharmacy without the miles, bringing a wave of natural pain relief and a drop in stress hormones.

Integrative Breathwork is an approach to breathwork and healing that evolved out of my Integrative Energy Healing sessions with clients and trainees. We believe that healing happens in the mind, body, and emotions so we can reconnect with the spiritual Self or Soul—that aspect of you that is whole. To do that, we practice a three-part breath with a focus on becoming more and more present—because the more present you become, the more you're able to see yourself from an empowered and objective perspective. By breathing with two inhales and one exhale, all through the mouth, you're likely to experience healthy signs that your nervous system is resetting within just a few minutes. For example, you may notice physical changes such as involuntary body movement, temperature shifts, spontaneous coughing, laughing, or crying.

Recent research (2023) from Stanford supports this approach. A study found that a simple double inhale followed by a long exhale—a pattern similar to the breathing we practice—calmed the nervous system faster than other techniques like "box breathing" (a technique using a different pattern of breath) (Zaccaro et al. 2023). In a study with eighty participants, this "cyclic sigh" helped people shift out of stress more quickly and naturally.

Integrative Breathwork also affects the mind and emotions. You might experience flashbacks or emotional outbursts, or connect with younger versions of yourself. Some people report having mystical experiences during breathwork where they connect with passed loved ones, experience a sense of oneness, and lose track of space and time.

Cross-cultural research shows that ritualized breath control has historically been used to induce non-ordinary states of consciousness in spiritual and healing contexts (Price 2011). Breathwork can complement all belief systems, offering a path to profound transformation through altered states of awareness by means of the very thing that all of us do all the time: breathe. When you engage in this kind of practice, it can be akin to what you might experience with psychedelics but without substances. These "non-ordinary" states support you to release deeply held emotional baggage from past trauma simply through breathing in a new way. In enabling you to access your subconscious mind, this type of breathwork helps you to see your life with detached objectivity to make more conscious choices that are unburdened by fear or shame.

WHY BREATHWORK IS ESSENTIAL

The way we breathe becomes the way we live. Most of us breathe in fight-or-flight mode—shallow and in our chest. This way of breathing sends signals to the brain and body to function as if you're under attack. When this happens, your body prioritizes short-term survival over long-term well-being: Your digestion slows, your vision narrows, your long-term thinking is reduced, and your immune system is suppressed. Shallow breathing increases your heart rate, and your body becomes flooded with stress chemicals, keeping you alert and ready for battle. Studies show that chronic chest-based breathing is associated with heightened stress reactivity, including increased cortisol and sympathetic arousal—whereas slow, diaphragmatic breathing produces the opposite effect, supporting parasympathetic activity and emotional regulation (Zaccaro et al. 2018). Though you're not aware of it, your breathing is setting off a chain reaction of downstream effects that increase stress, illness, and disease.

A regular breathwork practice has the opposite effect. While breathing through your nose is best for daily life, Integrative Breathwork helps you rapidly reset your nervous system to reverse the damage of being in stress mode for so long. Your immune system strengthens. Your capacity to digest increases—not just the food in your body, but in processing life's events. Your thinking becomes clearer, your nervous system resets, and your emotional capacity expands.

As Zen monk and peace activist Thích Nhất Hạnh wrote, mindful breathing is "the bridge" that allows the body to follow the mind into calm. With each round of breath, it's as if you're being rinsed and wrung out. That cleansing process turns down stressful thoughts, emotions, and sensations to give you access to your raw inner peace. With practice, the rest-and-digest state becomes your new normal. By simply changing the way you breathe, your whole life improves.

Now that you understand the foundational tenets, and you've seen how breathwork can help you reset your nervous system, let's explore what you'll find when you have the capacity to traverse your inner world.

CHAPTER 2

Your Inner World

YOU ARE NOT WHO YOU THINK YOU ARE. MUCH OF YOUR IDENTITY is a construction. Most of your personality, gender norms, beliefs, even likes and dislikes, were imposed upon you without you realizing it. A client of mine, let's call her Kimmie, always identified as a "nice person" who gave everything to her family, friends, and community. She was extremely put together and hardworking, and when we talked about making changes in her work and relationships, there was one thing she would not touch: anger. Even through her forced smiles, it was hard not to see that her identity of being a "nice person" was in direct conflict with feeling angry.

As a child, Kimmie was taught to value the way others felt over what was real for her. Eventually she became so disconnected from what she wanted and who she was that she buried herself in being of service to others. But one day, in a breathwork session, she met what she described as her "higher Self," a version of her that was totally accepting of all of her, even her rage. While in contact with her higher Self, she finally felt able to feel her anger, even hatred, for the first time in her life. She wailed and screamed as she released it. It poured out of her as she shook, screamed, and cried. She felt the rage that had been the painful tension under her anxiety for years.

She shared later that it was in those raw moments that she realized that most of her identity had been built on making her family happy. Her job, where she lived, and even her new boyfriend were all unconsciously chosen to make her family proud and amiable. Her whole life, she struggled with belonging and with pleasing her family. But when she came into contact with her unvarnished true "higher" Self, she realized that what she really longed for was belonging to herself. By making contact with the Self, what some might call the Soul, Kimmie found the freedom to be exactly as she was. And she was astonished to find that love was still there no matter what.

Kimmie's experience is universal. Most of your core beliefs were formed by what happened to you, what your caregivers modeled, and what was reflected to you about yourself. From life-changing traumas to everyday occurrences and lifetime achievements, you had hard-won evidence about what was real and possible for you. To string together the meaning of your life, you unconsciously created rules and formulas that inform your every action—even things like "being angry with someone means *I'm* not a good person." Unless you have spent years consciously questioning and remaking your assumptions, much of your life is run by a personality and set of beliefs that were built on the past unconscious choices of who you think you *should* be.

Who we are is not just something we decide—it's something shaped by the world around us. Research shows that both our genes and our environment work together to shape our identity from the very beginning (McAdams et al. 2022). It's hard to untangle what's truly "ours" from what we've absorbed. As sociologists Peter Berger and Thomas Luckmann (1991) have found, much of what we believe about ourselves is built through invisible social processes—family dynamics, cultural norms, the world we grow up in. Even the choices that feel the most personal often reflect expectations we've picked up without realizing it.

But it doesn't stop there, because you were born as a Soul in a baby's body. When you were born, you only had your DNA (and a birth experience) to inform your identity otherwise. You came in beaming, as the divine child. Full of life, bright-eyed, smiling and screaming too. Fully present to your needs, expressing without guilt or shame. From birth and through life and death, your Soul—or, in other words, your Self—emanates from within as a beacon of light guiding your steps back to wholeness—a wholeness so complete that there is no lack, separation, or individual identity. The Self is your personal experience of the impersonal infinite intelligence.

As a growing human, you assigned meaning to your subjective experience in order to locate yourself in the bigness of the unknown world. In that process, your consciousness became scattered and your psyche fractured into parts. The inner child, the artist, and more personas all emerge with their own wisdom, beliefs, and agendas. And these parts of your personality have little to no memory of an original Soul or Self. And so, you become stuck in an illusion of separateness and survival, grasping for wholeness and safety in the external world. Slowly, your preverbal Self-identity slips from memory completely. In life's overwhelming confusion, you forgot who you really were and where you came from.

The good news: Your true Self, your true identity, remained. And it's calling your parts back into coherence. Think of the last time you felt like the *real* you. Maybe it was after you left a toxic relationship, did a meditation retreat, or went on a long vacation, and you saw everything clearly. That process, of integrating back into wholeness, of feeling like the real you again, is Self-realization. And that is what we call healing—remembering who you really are.

This is why going within to explore your inner world is so life-altering. Everything you seek in the world to feel better, whole and complete, is only found within the Self. That feeling of being safe, okay, and at peace comes from being in touch with the inner sanctuary where your true Self resides. It was at those times early in your life that trauma made you believe that at your core you were not safe, whole, or okay. Those parts became burdened by the illusion of being separate, unsafe, and lacking. And that's why meeting and understanding your parts are essential to healing and transforming trauma. By healing the trauma-burdened aspects of your personality, you can remember and reidentify with the peace, joy, and infinite possibility that you had when you first entered the world. To begin that journey, one must be willing to go within, to question who they are and what they believe.

Going within takes real courage. Deep down, we all sense that if we do, our whole life will change. Much of what you'll uncover will be truths that you already knew but temporarily forgot—and that remembering brings great relief, because nothing compares to the feeling of coming home to yourself. I have experienced this firsthand. I have lived so many incarnations in this life, being a student, a model, an actress, a healer, and now an author. For a time I came to believe these identities were the fullest expression of me. But each time I pull back a new layer of who I thought I was, I free myself up to unfathomable possibilities of what more I can become. Over the years, few things have been more transformative than going within to question my deepest core beliefs of who I think I am. On the surface, everything seems "fine" about the way I see myself and the world, but as I've look deeper into my core personality traits, I've found that many of those beliefs or ways of identifying weren't working for me anymore. Can you think of any personal truths that you've lived by that may now be limiting or even harmful? Perhaps those beliefs are based on what you thought you should be, rather than what is true for you.

It took me years to realize that my hardworking personality was a trauma response. I grew up in hotels as a kid. We moved around the country to follow my mom's career, and by the time I was thirteen, I had moved at least eleven times. From all around Colorado to Florida, Colorado again, and then Texas. My mother worked her way up the corporate ladder from front desk associate to international hotel executive, and we all joined the effort to ensure her success. Sacrificing so much for work really stuck with me. From elementary school up until a few years ago, I took great pride in being a hard worker. My mom modeled that, and it became a huge part of my identity. My self-proclaimed elementary school slogan was "Hard work pays off." I was seven years old. Unbeknownst to me at the time, my life motto didn't stem from some universal truth, but from a general belief that was woven into my family history and socioeconomic standing. While hard work does pay off, when you need time to rest and reflect this motto can only get you so far. When I questioned this otherwise totally logical core belief, my whole life shifted. I went from working myself to death, and barely surviving, to working smarter and not harder so I could thrive.

This is why it is not only important to pause and reflect often, but to live in a way that allows you to check in on your subconscious beliefs and habits regularly and without guilt and shame. Do you want your relationships to follow the prototype of your parents? Or for your career to be based on the norms of your hometown? Without intentional inner exploration, it's likely that your adult life will be caught in a matrix between how your family treated you, how they treated each other, and what you saw in your community and in the media. It's safe to say that if you haven't traveled out of your comfort zone, spent time away from your family or childhood community, read many books outside of school, or sought deep healing and therapy, your approach to life is based on the generalized, limiting, and outdated beliefs of those who raised you and your surroundings growing up. And to keep it real, it likely means that you don't really know who you are or what you actually want, like, or dislike for yourself.

Note that I didn't say that this is necessarily bad or wrong. Because some of these core values have worked for you too. For most people, living by the principles of how you were raised is working just fine. For many, repeating these patterns from a family is generally tolerable, lovely even. In fact, we continue living our lives in these ways because they work for us. It's not until things *really* don't work for us that we start to question it. For others, subconsciously repeating the same patterns handed down from an alcoholic family member, for example, is not only unsustainable, but harmful.

But remember, we work on the premise that everything is for your use. No matter where you are or how you were raised, life's gifts and challenges are all the perfect ingredients for a masterpiece. The trauma, the love, the joy, the pain, and everything in between are all available to be of use for the Self's higher calling. It's through your healing journey that you get to have a personal, bodily experience of that redemption. Through healing, you get to realize how interconnected everything is. And through that process, everything in your life becomes Self-redeeming.

Let's take a moment to breathe. In through the nose for three counts, then hold for three seconds and exhale for three more. Do a few rounds as you reflect on the times in your life that you felt truly free or whole. Consider if these were moments when you were in touch with your inner wholeness—the Self.

YOUR INNER PARTS

Later, in the principle of integration, we'll talk about this at length. But for now, it's important to recognize that healing comes from reclaiming your parts so that you can remember who you really are. Because when you become aware of your parts and the programs they carry, you can integrate them. In turn, you make new meaning of your past, so that it no longer casts a shadow on your present. As we move through the seven principles together, you will come across your own inner parts. They might be of different ages, from a span of a few years to the age at which some part stopped growing as the result of a traumatic event, or even a joyful life change that it wanted to hold on to. These parts often have names and are usually willing to speak with you, with external guides, and with each other. They can also be felt in bodily sensations or through your emotions, and sometimes they may only communicate in these ways.

You might be most familiar with the inner child. The inner child that emerges can be in a particular stage of development, as with a younger part that still yearns to get what you once needed before moving on to the next stage of life. When overwhelmed by trauma, a younger part can become an exile. Exiled parts get isolated in the deep recesses of the unconscious to create distance from difficult feelings. While an exile's voice or ideas are hard to hear, its emotional energy builds up in the body. If not dealt with, the energy piles up, causing physical pain. Over time, these repressed emotions can cause depression and illness. Research has shown that this buildup isn't just emotional—it can take a physical toll. The landmark Adverse Childhood Experiences (ACE) Study, conducted by the Centers for Disease Control and Prevention (CDC) and Kaiser Permanente in the 1990s, found that heavy childhood trauma nearly triples the risk of developing autoimmune conditions and chronic pain later in life (Felitti et al. 1998). The effects can manifest in self-harming, self-sabotage, or drinking and drugging to numb the pain.

As a trauma response to the intensity, parts can emerge as "protectors," to keep you from feeling the pain of your original wounds. As if frozen in time, they tend to be based in fear. Going as far as blocking whole memories, protector parts grasp for power and control in order to protect and manage more vulnerable parts burdened by trauma. For example, if you have ever seen someone act out in a way that seems beyond their control, this may be an example of a protector grasping for power. Despite how messy things can get with our unintegrated parts, they emerge and stick around out of a desire to help. As Richard Schwartz (2021), Harvard professor and creator of Internal Family Systems (IFS), puts it, there are "no bad parts." While they might conflict with each other and may inadvertently cause harm, all of our parts are doing their absolute best to protect us and relieve our pain.

SO HOW DID THIS HAPPEN?

Trauma causes you to forget your innate wholeness. When you detach from your true Self in the wake of a traumatic event, you incur emotional and psychic wounds. The Centre for Addiction and Mental Health in Canada defines trauma as "the challenging emotional consequences that living through a distressing event can have for an individual." But that definition leaves out what happens in the body when the emotional trauma remains unresolved. After research that included surveys of over 17,000 people, the ACE Study documented this link when it looked at the effects of ten types of childhood trauma and adversities in life that one might encounter, such as neglect, abuse, or a parent's addiction. The study revealed that the more such events, or "ACEs," you've experienced, the higher the likelihood you'll have major negative health outcomes later in life, including heart conditions, cancer, or depression. Following are the original ten ACEs and the levels of trauma associated with them.

The Ten Original ACEs from the CDC-Kaiser Study

Abuse

1. Physical Abuse
2. Emotional Abuse
3. Sexual Abuse

Neglect

4. Physical Neglect
5. Emotional Neglect

Household Dysfunction

6. Mental Illness in Household
7. Substance Abuse in Household
8. Mother Treated Violently
9. Divorce or Separation of Parents
10. Incarcerated Household Member

ACE Scores and Outcomes

Having four or more ACEs significantly increases risk for:

- Depression (4.5 × higher risk)
- Alcoholism (7 × higher risk)
- Drug abuse (10 × higher risk)
- Suicide attempts (12 × higher risk)
- Heart disease (2 × higher risk)
- Cancer (2 × higher risk)
- Stroke (2.5 × higher risk)
- Chronic Obstructive Pulmonary Disease (3.5 × higher risk)

The CDC has updated the study at various times to include more factors:

Community/Environmental ACEs

- Experiencing racism, discrimination, or bullying
- Living in an unsafe neighborhood
- Witnessing violence outside the home
- Experiencing collective trauma (natural disasters, pandemics, etc.)
- Housing instability/homelessness
- Food insecurity
- Growing up in poverty
- Foster care system involvement

I saw an example of how this kind of trauma can play out with one of my clients, whom I'll call Sam. Sam's family struggled with periods of homelessness during his childhood. As an adult, Sam developed chronic health issues and had difficulty maintaining close relationships. Through our work together, Sam discovered how different parts of himself had emerged to help him survive those early experiences—a hypervigilant part that was always preparing for the worst, and another part that pushed people away before they could abandon him. These parts had protected young Sam when he needed them. But as an adult, they were keeping him from the connection and peace he desperately wanted. Though he hadn't previously realized it, Sam's childhood experiences had been setting him up for a future of mental and physical health issues. By embarking on a process of healing within the psyche, he began to unwind his childhood trauma.

According to the US federal government's Substance Abuse and Mental Health Services Administration, nearly two in three individuals under the age of sixteen have experienced at least one form of trauma. If that is you, I believe there will be a day when you can say that you have made new meaning of what happened to you. And though I wouldn't wish the pain that you have experienced upon anyone, I know that trauma can be transformed. My personal healing process has proven this to me. Despite having an ACE score of eight out of ten, I was able to transcend my fate of abuse, alcoholism, illness, and addiction. I believe that this was made possible by healing the parts of myself that unconsciously held trauma. Diagnosed with post-traumatic stress disorder (PTSD) years ago, I was once an anxious person, with all kinds of physical health issues to boot. Without the help of pharmaceutical medications, I have come to a point where I am no longer suffering those effects on a daily basis. That's not to say that if you're taking medications that's a bad thing or that you should stop. What I'm saying is that through the practices and principles I share in this book, I've been able to resolve traumatic experiences that went beyond what doctors and therapists said could be healed. I was told that I was an anxious personality type, genetically prone to anxiety, and had "inexplicable" physical health issues that I would have to endure or that needed to be treated with prescription medication. It turns out that I was having psychosomatic issues that were being triggered by the unresolved trauma of my past. This holistic understanding changed everything for me, as many of those issues have been resolved since I started doing many of the healing practices that I share with you in this book.

Health isn't the only reason we do this kind of healing. This work affects the way our lives feel in the day-to-day. When we go through something painful, it doesn't just live in our memory—it lives in our body, too. Without realizing it, we can find ourselves repeating old patterns, even when they hurt us. Dr. Bessel van der Kolk and colleagues (2014), a leading voice in trauma research, described how trauma can get "wired in" to the way we react, both emotionally and physically. Later studies have suggested that these memories often stay buried in our bodies, more like feelings than stories. When stress shows up again, it can pull us right back into those familiar, painful places even when it seems like a regular day—not because we want to suffer, but because, on some deep level, we're trying to find a way through it.

These aren't just soft spots from our wounded past, but relationship dynamics and daily behaviors that we unconsciously repeat. For example, for much of my young adult life, I was a rigid person who trusted no one. Self-isolation became my only safe place. I would not allow myself to be vulnerable enough to trust another person. And like so many of my clients, I began to attract the same kinds of relationships that I was trying to avoid. Without realizing it, I would only choose friends and lovers that ended up mirroring the relationships I had in my family of origin. It wasn't until I healed the original pain and explored why I believed no one could be trusted that my relationships begin to reflect the wholesome kinship that I longed for.

Long-held beliefs can be likened to computer programs. The belief that I couldn't trust anyone became an underlying program that worked in my subconscious mind. Such programs can act as the nonemotional operating systems of our parts. They tend to come with a set of beliefs and emotional attachments that arose in response to an event or a series of correlating events. Similar to an AI bot that performs certain actions in given circumstances, our programs are put in place to automate how we operate within assumed circumstances. These totally unconscious guiding principles become the underlying motivations that lead the way in our daily lives without us even realizing it.

Objective, and neither good nor bad, programs can be upgraded at any time. Like apps on your phone or computer, they will cause dysfunction when they become outdated—but in this case, dysfunction for the parts of the Self and for the Self's ecosystem. When your programs update, so do your beliefs, motivations, and daily habits. Such updates can be a watershed moment in your life. That's what happened for me when I challenged the underlying program that said people can't be trusted.

It's helpful to know that programs are not parts, but that most parts are run by programs, and programs can get updated with relative ease. Some programs are passed down nonverbally, by how your family shows love, or through informal family mottos, like "Life is hard." These become codes by which you live your life, and they can determine how you see the world. Some of our programs are helpful, like not having to think about how to get dressed. Some are not so helpful, like unconsciously being afraid of people of a certain color or background.

Our minds and bodies aren't fixed—they're designed to adapt. A 2023 study found that the brain has circuits built not just to form habits, but to break them when we engage with new experiences (Smith et al. 2023). With awareness, old patterns can be updated, and the emotional weight they carry begins to lift. Each shift strengthens your connection to the Self and opens space for transformation. Breaking them requires that we wake up to our underlying programs to consciously work with them. When updating programs directly, you can work quickly to support your parts in seeing the bigger picture from a more up-to-date perspective. Once your parts have been relieved of old programs, the past emotional meaning shifts, giving you the ability to see and feel in new ways that you never imagined. Each time you upgrade the programs that have been unconsciously in place, you strengthen the connection with the Self. In later chapters, we'll work together in this way to transform trauma into wisdom, love, and compassion.

THE SHADOW

I know how scary it can be to face what you have been through. Most of us were taught that it's best to leave the past in the past. But leaving the past unresolved will only ensure that it will follow you like a shadow wherever you go. It's likely that you have heard people refer to their shadow, and often the connotation is bad. They typically allude to their shadow being a dangerous part of themselves. The part they better not let out, lest they behave badly. But the shadow isn't bad. The shadow is made up of the parts of yourself that remain unintegrated because you fear, deny, forbid, or reject them. And this includes what might otherwise be called your "light"—the gifts, talents, and strengths that you fear and suppress as much as your wounded parts.

Let's say that in your family you were the golden child, a dysfunctional family role where a child is elevated in value to uphold an ideal of perfection by narcissistic parents. In this example of an unhealthy family dynamic, perhaps your artistic talent was obsessively venerated by your father, but your mother became jealous and would "cut you down to size" so that you wouldn't think too highly of yourself. After a few years, you might, as a young child, start to push away your artistic talents, just to keep the peace. In a case like this, your natural gifts may have come to symbolize danger and disenfranchisement rather than joy and freedom. As you grew up, that suppressed inner artist became hungrier, creating chaos as it tried to express your artistic potential. What was once your most celebrated light has now become your secret shadow.

Over the years I have seen this story play out in seemingly unrelated ways. At first, it's hard to see how one's suppressed inner power might take the form of relentless cheating or the inability to keep a stable job. Often, this suppressed part creates not only drama, but also a host of health issues. From stomach problems to migraines, depression, and even infertility, many of us are suffering from issues that doctors and therapists can't get to the bottom of. But I have seen how they can be directly related to the shadow parts of ourselves, the parts that dare to express themselves in any way that's possible. The health problems are real. Medicine and therapy can help, and even save your life. And, time and again, I have seen mysterious ailments disappear, both in myself and in clients, when the unowned inner shadow is integrated.

Modern studies are beginning to confirm what many have felt for years. Our bodies often carry what our minds try to forget. Studies show that when people work through hidden emotional wounds, physical symptoms often improve—even when traditional medicine couldn't explain them. A review of twenty-three studies (Abbass et al. 2009) found that short-term therapies addressing buried emotional conflicts helped ease chronic physical symptoms, and that the improvements tended to last. Other research found that releasing repressed emotions can help with conditions such as irritable bowel syndrome, fibromyalgia, and chronic headaches. And one study even found that bringing hidden emotional experiences into the light led to healthier levels of inflammation and stress hormones. Healing the parts of us we once pushed away doesn't just feel better, it can ripple outward into the body, too.

When the shadow is reclaimed, you become a more holistically healthy adult. The person in the earlier example can go on to create great art in healthy and empowering ways. Making friends with your shadow can end up changing the trajectory of your life. And many, including myself, have begun to see dramatic improvements in their health as well. While working with the seven principles, you will encounter the shadow of your inner world, uncovering forgotten parts, talents, memories, and wounds as you explore. In healing, we work to uncover the painful experiences of our past so that we can recover any of our parts that are stuck in an outdated reality. In bringing them into the light, so to speak, you make new meaning of the past by bringing your parts into the present. Because so much of the shadow has been kept out of your awareness, most of the work is simply about becoming conscious, so you can update the way these parts of you see things.

THE SELF

We've talked a lot about the Self already, but before we move on to the principles, I want to make sure we are on the same page about how central it is to the healing process. Some people call it their inner voice. Across cultures and traditions, this idea has always been with us—known as Brahman in Vedanta, the Tao in Taoism, the Spirit in indigenous teachings, or simply the infinite intelligence of nature itself. The Self is both personal and universal. When I encounter this version of myself, I innately understand that at my core, I am infinite, timeless, genderless, without opinions or conditionality. Experiencing this as my identity is so far from a logical experience that words are futile. Words cannot even begin to explain what that experience is like. But I'll try; it is our personal experience of oneness. The Self in you is the same Self in me. The Self is where we all meet, where we experience oneness, but from different bodily vantage points.

Experiences of oneness and expanded self-awareness aren't just ancient ideas, they're showing up in modern science too. Research by neuroscientists Andrew Newberg and Eugene d'Aquili (2000) has found that during deep meditation and contemplative states, the brain shifts in measurable ways. Their studies, published in the *Journal of Consciousness Studies*, show that activity in the parietal lobe, the part of the brain that normally draws the line of separation between you and the world around you—goes quiet in these states. This matches the feeling many people describe of boundaries dissolving and identity expanding. Similar patterns show up in psychedelic-assisted therapy research at Johns Hopkins University, where participants have reported "mystical-type experiences" of unity and timelessness that often lead to lasting positive change (Griffiths et al. 2008). Science can't fully explain the nature of the Self, but what it can show is that these experiences are real, that they are repeatable, and that they can deeply transform the way we live.

Thankfully, the Self has been experienced by many others who have tried to put the ineffable into words, too. Richard Schwartz (2021), Harvard professor and the creator of IFS, speaks of the Self as "an essence of calm, clarity, compassion, and connectedness." In his book *Vedanta Treatise* (2014), the Indian swami and philosopher A. Parthasarathy says that the Self is "the abode of absolute peace and bliss." Author Robert Greene speaks about what he calls the "true self" at length in *Mastery* (2012), saying, "Your true self does not speak in words of banal phrases. Its voice comes from deep within you, from the substrata of your psyche, from something embedded physically within you." And in one of my favorite books of all time, *Women Who Run with the Wolves* (1992), author Clarissa Pinkola Estés says, "The Soul, the Self, knows what it needs to heal itself. The challenge is to silence the mind long enough to let the Soul speak."

In this framework you will come to have your own personal relationship with what we will refer to as the capital "S" Self to differentiate it from the lowercase "s" self, the ego, or personality. The ego, in this context, is the collective personality of your inner parts. It is the intangible aspect of what makes you human, as it is purely focused on survival and needs being met. Your parts split off from the Self because they believe they don't have what they need to survive. This is a key characteristic to remember about the difference between your Self and your parts. The Self does not need anything. The Self opens and includes. The ego, on the other hand, denies, separates, and negates, because it believes in lack. The ego has rules and wants to keep you safe at all costs. The Self is affirmative and all permitting, while remaining interested in your well-being.

An extreme example of this distinction can be seen in situations where the ego is terrified by thoughts arising from the parts, such as "I should just kill myself." At first blush, we would imagine that we would want to avoid such thoughts, because of the harm to our bodies that could follow if we were to listen. In the case of suicidal ideation, the ego tends to rise up to suppress such thoughts. Logically, out of fear, the ego condemns the part that feels this way, so as to not allow the thought to go further, into harm. It is a logical protection strategy. The Self, however, is loving, nonjudgmental, and without fear. The Self knows there is no need to fix or condemn the part that sees suicide as the best option.

Instead, the Self listens and lovingly witnesses what the part is feeling, because it is through love and acceptance that things shift out of fear and despair. Without acting to "fix" the feeling, the Self helps this part of you feel seen and less alone. The Self knows that the parts are unaware of what they really seek, and of what it takes to be whole again. By allowing the Self to come forward and be with this part that yearns for wholeness, you can help this part wake up from its illusion of separation and lack. And while it may take time to integrate this realization into every aspect of one's life, this once isolated and heavily burdened part might finally be ready to rejoin its true source of aliveness, the Self, while still living in physical form. I have witnessed this very act of love help the parts that thought death was the only way to end the pain and to be whole again. While it's best to have the help of a trauma-informed professional when facing this kind of challenge, because there is much more practice and integration that goes into this kind of recovery, perhaps you can see how this process is often counterintuitive to what most schools of thought teach.

When you grow the capacity to do this kind of inner work, even the scariest and most intrusive thoughts start to tell a different story. Now you can see things from the perspective of a higher Self rather than from your fears. The Self has a quiet way of transforming whatever it meets. If you're new to this kind of unconditional love, it's likely that a skilled practitioner can help exhibit that for you. A guide who has learned to become attuned to their own unconditional inner love can help you retell the story of what has happened to you through the eyes of love as well. This retelling is not delusional; in fact, it's the exact opposite. Rather than bypassing or avoiding unresolved or challenging issues, healing with the Self allows you to see beyond the fog of fear. From this higher view, it often becomes easier to work with what you've lived through, rather than feeling trapped inside it. The Self helps us to build the bridge, and then to have the faith to cross that bridge, by making everything we have been through for our use.

The principles in this book are meant to help you encircle past trauma with the awareness and love of the Self. By doing so for even a moment, you can begin to resolve traumatic events into historical facts that open the door to deeper understanding. I share this because it has been true in my own experience and in the experiences of many people I've worked with directly. My own process reflects the very words and work that I'm offering here.

Outside of a healing environment, if you've never encountered this level of deep restoration, I understand that it may seem unrealistic to suggest that one can resolve even the most painful traumas. It might sound impossible. It might even seem to suggest a dismissal of what happened or a forgiveness that feels undeserved. But I have witnessed the Self at work over and over again as people use these principles to find real change in their lives.

These principles are grounded in the idea that resolution often begins with what happened in you, not only what happened to you. We cannot always control what life brings, but healing can be possible when we tend to our inner world in the wake of things. Only you can nurture this inner landscape—and as you do, your inner ecology can begin to thrive.

As I work with clients I guide them through a breathwork practice. They breathe deeply: two inhales and one exhale, all through the mouth, as described in Chapter 1. Step by step, they go deeper and deeper into themselves. Sometimes, I'll ask clients to tell me what they see. Some describe a desert, a luminous heavenly landscape, a jungle, or a dark void. I ask them to feel for their Self, often with no description of what that even means or how, and yet they know what to do. Something starts to appear naturally. Perhaps they just feel it or see it far off in the distance. As they get closer, their faces and bodies reveal their awe. I can see and feel that something magnificent is happening within them.

One time, a client became very scared when I asked her to feel for her Self. She moved slowly, getting closer and closer to what she described aloud as a ball of light. As she felt the warmth, the light became a mirror. I witnessed her face shift from trepidation to deep recognition. When I asked her what she saw, she sobbed, at a loss for words. Finally she said, "It's me. The light is me. I am the Self. And I am Love."

A MAP OF YOUR INNER WORLD

There are numerous parts to ourselves that make up our internal world. Each part plays a role in our daily lives, so it's important to get to know them. Let's briefly cover the core parts that make up our inner world. Check in with a breath after reading each one to see if anything comes to mind, and then make a note to revisit it later.

THE SELF (CORE IDENTITY)

The Self is the spacious awareness that can hold joy, fear, rage, and shame without being defined by any of them. It is your true identity, whole and wise, and it remains steady even as the other parts shift and change within it.

INNER CHILD(REN) (DEVELOPMENTAL PARTS)

These are the parts that "broke off" between birth and the age of about thirteen. Some of them reflect different versions of you, like the playful, curious child who loved to explore. Others may represent parts of you that never had the chance to express themselves, like a "bad kid" who wanted to rebel in a strict home. These parts carry innocence, energy, imagination, and creativity. When wounded, they may become burdened by fear, guilt, or shame and lose the connection to their original spark.

INNER TEENAGER(S)

These parts emerge between the ages of thirteen and nineteen. They often seek freedom, independence, connection, and purpose. When they're healthy, they bring boldness and adventure. When they're weighed down in pain, they may act out in chaos, defiance, or through rigid control. They can become like internal revolutionaries, pushing back against anything that feels unfair or restrictive.

PROTECTORS

Protectors step in to keep your more vulnerable parts safe. They may show up as perfectionism, a desire for people-pleasing, high achievement, or emotional numbness. Some protectors act as managers, using strategies such as working constantly, controlling food intake, or staying busy. Others take the form of inner critics who believe their criticism is necessary to keep you safe. These parts are often the most active ones in your day-to-day life, as their role is to protect what's most tender and unconscious.

INTERNALIZED PARTS

These parts are shaped by people or influences from the outside world. They might include:

- **Inner Parents/Family:** These are based on caregivers from your childhood, or the idealized family you wished you had. They often act as protectors, repeating beliefs and behaviors you learned early on. In some cases of abuse, the inner family member may be a harmful internalized influence as well.
- **Introjects:** These parts carry shame, guilt, or trauma. They may repeat harmful patterns, trying to protect you by keeping you quiet, small, or out of harm's way. At times, an introject could be the internalized perpetrator, abuser, or victimizer from traumatic situations or relationships.
- **Collective Unconscious:** The collective unconscious is shaped by media, culture, or cultural archetypes. It may show up in the form of inner guides or the false self you wear in public to fit in. It's Beyoncé's Sasha Fierce, but it may also be represented by an archetype like the devil. The collective unconscious supplies guides of all sorts.
- **Healer/Helper:** This part knows how to bring you back to balance. It may soothe you with music, lead you outside for fresh air, or tell you to rest. It's often a source of comfort and wisdom. But like all other parts, it, too, can become imbalanced. It might use isolation or avoidance in the name of self-care, or shut down completely when overwhelmed. At its best, the healer helps you regulate, repair, and return to a sense of inner safety.

PART 2

The Seven Principles

CHAPTER 3

The Principle of Presence

When I think about how I have overcome the abuse of my childhood, I know that none of this would have been possible if I hadn't learned to become present. Especially with really tough stuff I'd rather ignore and push away. I wouldn't have had the capacity to hold the level of fear and powerlessness that I experienced in those harrowing moments of my younger years if I had been in my everyday state of mind. But because of breathwork, I had a tool to expand my capacity to face what pained me.

Learning how to become deeply present enabled me to face what seemed too unbearable to revisit. Counter to what I once believed, it was bearing witness to what happened to me as a child that made it possible to reinterpret those situations in a way that empowered me. No longer a traumatized child caught in an overwhelming situation, I was an adult who was able to use a deeply present state to face a terrible trauma with a new perspective. In doing do, I set myself free. And because I have gone to the depths of these painful experiences, as well as having helped many clients do the same, I know that we all have the same opportunity to transmute the traumatic events of our past into the transformative turning points of our present. The principle of presence is the first step to how you can experience this kind of deep healing too.

Presence is one of the most powerful tools we have for healing and transformation. It is the state of fully engaging the current moment without judgment or resistance. It involves bringing complete awareness to your thoughts, your emotions, your bodily sensations, and the world around you in real time. Through presence, you access the part of yourself that witnesses your experiences without getting caught up in them. It's the ability to simultaneously witness and objectively experience your emotions, thoughts, and bodily sensations. This point of view is how the Self experiences your life. Found in the right here, right now, presence is available to you at any moment of your daily life if you're willing to pay attention. Because we are so rarely present, especially these days, we forget how profound this state can be.

THE WITNESS

To understand how presence works, it's crucial to begin with the concept of the Witness. Witness, in this context, is capitalized, as it is interchangeable with the Self, because this is what your higher Self does your entire life. One of the most important concepts in ancient Vedanta, the ancient philosophy behind Buddhism and Hinduism, is *Sakshi*, the concept of the eternal observer within who witnesses all thoughts, actions, and things without being affected by them.

Imagine a movie playing on a screen. Now imagine that your mind is the screen, and your thoughts and experiences are the lines and scenes of the movie. The Witness is the audience watching the story play out. It recognizes the faces and the story but knows it's just a movie. From this perspective, you start to pick up on the fact that you are not your thoughts, and you are much more than your body. Just like when you watch a good film, although you care about what happens to the characters, at the end of the day you know it's not real. Presence is the mechanism that gives you this detached, objective view. When you spend enough time in this judgment-free space, you begin to remember that you are not only the watcher of this movie but the executive producer, too. By practicing presence, you wake up from playing a role and remember that you can change the story anytime.

Every human being has a Self that has witnessed everything that has ever happened. The Self is not afraid. The Self does not judge or pity. The Self knows that everything has a purpose and a use. You gain this perspective when you become deeply present. It's a superpower. When you courageously face whatever is unfolding in the moment, you begin to see clearly. When you see through the eyes of the Witness, you take your power back and see things from a mile-high view. All it takes is just a few minutes of your undivided attention.

But when you lose touch with the Witness, you become attached to being the character whose story is bound to the rules of a script that your family, community, and culture wrote for you. Presence requires that you detach from identifying as the character. To become objective is to let go of expectations, judgment, or intervention. It's similar to how you shake off a bad dream when you wake up: Presence is how you realize who and what you really are. But you can't just think it, it's a state of being.

Let's practice this right now.

Close your eyes and sing "Happy Birthday" to yourself.

Go ahead and try it in your mind: Sing the whole song inside of your mind. Who was listening? Who heard you sing to yourself? That's the Witness.

PRESENCE: A TOOL TO DETACH FROM THOUGHTS

Presence has an expansive and layered quality. The more you focus on what is unfolding in real time, the wider your perception and capacity to be in the Witness state of mind. You become more present by focusing on what you notice, layer by layer, with each of your senses. Breathe. Start with listening to all the sounds in the moment as you read: Perhaps you hear music playing, people talking, birds chirping, cars passing, sirens blaring in the background, or even your breath. With just a few seconds of attentive listening, you start to feel more in your body, a sign that you're more present. This is a great way to begin pulling back the layers of presence, because the sounds in your external environment are akin to the thoughts in your head. At first it's noise, but listen deeper, and it becomes information. Deeper still, and the sounds start to fade altogether.

You aren't trying to make the world silent or less chaotic. Presence is about noticing the noise and chaos and expanding your capacity to include it rather than denying it or pushing it away.

See the metaphor here? This goes for anything in life. As you allow yourself to be with the sounds of the external world, your window of tolerance expands to gently hold more of what you become aware of. To "be with" means to be present without action. By becoming present to your mind's chatter, or to the horns honking on the street, you notice how external stimuli affect you internally. But with presence, you don't need to judge or change the external world to feel better or at peace. Rather than trying to control your mind or surroundings, you can use presence to witness, open, and notice them without judging yourself or others. Instead of the sirens outside being a distraction, they act as a flash point in the flow of time, now simply indicating that you are present with what is unfolding.

Ever notice how, when you feel stressed, a loud noise or unkind word can deeply trigger you? When you are able to detach from the sounds in the external world, you have a larger capacity to handle the flow of thoughts in your mind. When you're less agitated, you're better able to witness the thoughts that you previously had to ignore just to get through your day. Detaching from your thoughts is like watching them pass like clouds across the sky. Remember how you heard yourself sing "Happy Birthday"? This is the same thing you can do with any thought that passes through your mind. Not all your thoughts are true or even coming from you. By witnessing your thoughts and holding your awareness with your undivided attention, you'll be able to enter a new layer of presence very quickly, and you'll gain enough distance to catch what is behind the thoughts—the emotions and beliefs. Hold your attention long enough, and you'll inevitably start feeling emotions and sensations you didn't realize were related. Now you open to a flow of information that was once hidden within plain sight.

PRESENCE TO RELEASE SUPPRESSED EMOTIONS

You have a body so that you can feel and experience your life. But most people spend so much time in their heads that they cut themselves off from really living. In its purest form, emotions are information: They are meant to transmit messages between the brain and the body, to be utilized and then released. Some emotions have such a charge in your psyche that you suppress them rather than allowing the information to circulate. With nowhere to go and nothing to do, the pressure of the withheld emotional energy can become stress, pain, and even illness. Presence is the mechanism that gently lifts the pressure valve of suppressed emotional energy, freeing the underlying information to become useful wisdom and physical relief.

Feeling emotions is twofold, as it involves not just emotional states, but the bodily sensations that come with them. When you go further into presence, beyond the thoughts of the mind, you experience how emotions can be held in physical sensations. It's one thing to witness your thoughts objectively; it takes more practice to remain detached when you feel your emotions. This next step in presence is where most people stop, because they start to actually feel their feelings for the first time in a while. I'm flagging this for you now: Most people are terrified to feel their feelings. This is because there are a host of emotions that you were taught were dangerous, and, in turn, were never taught how to express.

There is no emotion that's inherently bad; each one carries information, even if it's uncomfortable to feel. And yet every family and every culture has a blacklist of emotions that are considered unacceptable. Perhaps in your family anger was not allowed even when it was necessary. Or perhaps anger was so common that the emotional state of being satisfied or at peace felt inauthentic. No matter what family you came from or what societal norms you grew up with, when you practice presence you'll find that there are certain emotions you have subconsciously roped off to keep yourself from feeling. And those feelings have powerful energy. The ones that have the strongest charge and will do the most damage are the ones you continue to resist.

Even the most admirable emotions can be terrifying to feel. If you grew up in a downcast home or community, it was likely that being a happy child was incongruent with the environment and culture. You may not realize that emotions like joy, curiosity, and even bliss have been off-limits for decades because you shut them down as a child to fit in. Now, when joy or excitement comes up, you unknowingly experience it as anxiety (withheld excitement), or a threat to belonging, and you can only uncover those unconscious archaic beliefs by being present as you feel them. When you do, your emotions inform you of their preassigned meaning.

As you move deeper into presence in breathwork, for example, you might experience actual physical pain. That's because body pains are the epicenters of long-suppressed emotions, so tapping into body tension is the most direct path to uncovering the emotions that have been suppressed the longest. When you practice breathwork, the habits that you have in place to suppress those emotions tend to surface quickly, leaving you with bodily sensations that feel foreign or that may be reminiscent of a traumatic or painful isolated event. Your breath might become shallow, and your heart rate and pain might increase in the body, as if you were doing something wrong. For a few seconds, totally unconsciously, you might resist all of this. If you can, allow yourself to be present with that, too; the emotions and bodily sensations will pass through, and the experience will leave you with information and relief.

You must feel the emotion in your body to get this information; it is not something you can think about to access. So whatever comes with the experiencing, like feelings of shame or fear, try to be open to as well. It's a matter of opening yourself up to accept and embody what you have otherwise deemed unacceptable so that you can see what might be on the other side. Only then can the emotion, and all the correlating energy, memories, and beliefs, be freed up as useful material. This requires a great deal of presence, but with adequate support, anyone can do this in minutes. And when you do, the meaning you assigned to it will shift.

Can you imagine how much anger you hold in your body? Think back to the first story I shared at the beginning of the book. The scream that I couldn't let out still lingered. I didn't even realize it, but it was there like a ghost haunting me for decades. I'm sure you understand—because you have your own hauntings that are likely sending you alerts as you read this. I know that you have them too, because you are alive, and living requires that you've suffered at some point in life.

Perhaps you haven't experienced severe trauma, but you have suffered, whether you remember it or not. It's what you do with that suffering that determines the life you live. The emotions you experienced in those difficult moments are the building blocks for the person you've become. In painful experiences that you endured, the only way forward was survival. Perhaps you had to abandon the version of you that experienced that kind of pain, because you didn't know how to relieve it. But that part of you remains, and becoming deeply present is one of the ways that you can heal.

HOW TO HEAL WITH PRESENCE

By detaching from the fear and negative labeling of your emotions, you can see your beliefs and subsequent actions from a higher perspective. One of my clients, whom I'll call "Jen," came to me when she was having a hard time getting pregnant. She had been hoping to do so for nearly two years and was in perfect health. Her doctors couldn't get to the bottom of her infertility because all her tests came back great. In a last push to get to the bottom of her struggle, she decided to explore an alternative method: breathwork.

From the first few minutes of the practice, Jen began to sense a correlation between her career and her fertility. Lately, the work she'd loved had felt more like a job and less like the passion that she'd started out with. As she started to become present with her emotions, she was overcome by anger, a feeling that she otherwise felt too guilty to admit. She realized that she was angry with family members, because they had come to rely on her creative talents to cover a large portion of the bills. Feeling this rage toward her husband, in particular, along with guilt over her success, she realized that these were feelings she had never let herself fully acknowledge.

As Jen became more present, she began to release the anger. She was astounded by the subsequent realization that her feelings of guilt over her success had led her to refuse help from others. She was overcompensating for her success by taking on the bulk of the family's financial burdens despite their protests. By breathing into this revelation, she noticed her fears about having a child. If she were to keep refusing support, because of the guilt over her success, she wouldn't be able to hold being a mom, too. Deep down, she felt that her long-standing belief that her success was unfair to others would make motherhood unsustainable. With great self-compassion, she felt into the guilt and decided it was time to let go of this belief that her talent was unfair. This allowed her to see that it was safe and healthy for her to accept support from others, rather than feeling that she owed so much to them.

When we finished the breathwork, she was ready to accept help. She now firmly believed that she deserved support even when she was thriving. She admitted that the reason her passion had felt like a nine-to-five job for the past year was that she was working so hard to ensure that everyone else was okay with her success. She was performing struggle, so it didn't look so easy. But now, she was ready to let all that go. A few months later, I got an email. My client was pregnant with her first child.

Jen realized that deep down, she didn't want to have kids until she changed how she was showing up in her work and with her family. She used the power of presence to wake up to the beliefs that she had never even questioned. Without entering into deep states of presence, your ego will keep creating the same challenges and patterns encoded in your subconscious mind by your family, friends, and culture. But by using it as a tool for deep introspection, you gain the objectivity that you need to shape a life of your own choosing.

One way to understand the interplay between objective awareness and the personality ego is to look at mobile devices, which we've built on our idea of the brain. Like an iPhone, your psyche has an operating system, with programs (a set of beliefs) and apps (automated tools and habits) that run your daily life behind the scenes in your subconscious mind. Many of the programs running in the background were "installed" when you were a kid.

The human brain runs most of your daily activities on autopilot, so you don't have to keep relearning simple activities like using the toilet, brushing your teeth, or putting on clothes. But those mundane daily activities aren't the only things on autopilot. Unless you have consciously uncovered, uninstalled, or updated these "programs," some beliefs may remain in place long after they're useful to you. For example, your beliefs about money today might be what you were taught when you were a young child. How you react to a partner who says something you don't like is also automated and likely from a code written years or even decades ago.

While most of your daily interactions with yourself and others are simple, those unconscious actions can quickly add up to a life that you didn't consciously choose. Like my client Jen, who untangled a web of outdated beliefs when she finally let herself be present to her guilt and anger, you can use the principle of presence to wake up to subconscious beliefs that need your attention. And just like a device that goes offline to do a whole system update, you can use deep states of sustained presence to update your entire OS.

PRESENCE IS HOW YOU MEET YOUR SELF

I've spoken at length about the Self. Presence is how you gain the vantage point of the Witness. But presence is also how you can meet the Self as if it were a long-lost loved one. The Self is pure love, joy, and peace. But this is something that most people reject or ignore when I first tell them. Perhaps because it sounds so woo-woo or because it's something they don't remember ever experiencing. But when you were a young child, it's likely that you were in touch with the Self all the time. I remember being about seven years old, and for no reason at all, sometimes at recess, I would laugh and laugh at anything and everything. I remember enjoying myself for hours, smiling so hard that my face hurt. That's the innocence of a child who is connected to their Self. We see it in puppies and kittens, too, and we can't look away, because a part of us yearns to be that free. Thankfully, with the principle of presence, you can be.

I am always amazed by how naturally my clients can meet their Self by practicing presence. I work with families and sometimes spend time in sessions with my clients' children. On one of these occasions, when guiding a tween through a breathwork practice and visualization, I asked her to imagine that she was driving the car of her dreams (something she was too young to do in real life). I went on to ask her to imagine that there were people in the car with her that she needed to speak with. When I noticed her scrunching up her face, I knew some strong emotions were coming to the surface. I talked her through the breathwork, reminding her that she was safe to continue breathing and feeling her feelings. We went from person to person in the car, speaking to members of her family and sharing things with them that she had wanted to share but had been too afraid to say.

What happened next blew my mind. Noting that she was in a deep state of total presence, I asked her what was going on that was starting to make her so emotional. "Who is there in the car now?" I asked her. Unable to speak or keep her tears in, she pointed to herself. "Oh, you are in the car with another version of you?" I asked. She nodded her head. "What are you saying to yourself right now?" I asked several times. "I love you!" she blurted out as fast as possible. In amazement, I thought I would test the waters further. "Oh, is that your higher Self, telling you that she loves you?" Now, my tween client looked totally overwhelmed by what I can only describe as all-encompassing love. It seemed as if her young mind was so enraptured by the love she was experiencing from her Self that all she could do was cry as she smiled. I was astounded: The Self is the most natural and real aspect of who we are, and this young girl was more proof that this is universal.

If you're interested in experiencing this kind of love and acceptance, but question whether what I'm talking about is real, that's okay. You don't have to believe me or in the concept of an inner higher Self to experience it. All that is needed from you is to be open and willing. I and millions of other people have used the following practice to access the objective state of presence that many have described as "fifteen years of therapy in just one session." The three-part breathwork sequence that we will do in the following practice has been proven by science and tested for thousands of years. Try it out for yourself so that you can sync up with what presence has to offer you.

Practicing Presence

As you may have noticed by now, breathwork is one of the most powerful ways to access presence. Breath is the direct line from the body to your inner voice and wisdom. Indigenous cultures have practiced intentional breathing for centuries to connect with the Self and affect the mind and body. And science is now proving its ability to regulate emotions and create altered states. The three-part breathwork practice introduced later in this chapter can bring a busy mind into an acutely felt presence within just a few minutes. When practiced for a few minutes uninterrupted, this intentional breath pattern can bring up previously unnoticed physical sensations, emotions, and mental chatter. You may tear up or notice your body twitch or shudder. Breathwork relies on the body's intelligence to do what it knows to do. The body knows when to cry, when to modulate oxygen intake, and when to become calm or engage in release. By becoming present in your body, you let your body do its healing work.

It's important to check in with yourself to ensure that this practice is right for you at this time. While this practice is self-led, it can bring about intense emotions and painful memories and might be best explored with a trauma-informed trained professional. If you have complex trauma, have PTSD, or struggle with addiction, I highly recommend working with a professional before doing the following practice on your own. If you are pregnant, it may be best not to do this practice in your third trimester. If you have any heart conditions or epilepsy, you might want to be under medical supervision.

If you are currently in a crisis or feel emotionally overwhelmed, please reach out to a helpline or mental health support service for immediate assistance. Resources like Find a Helpline (https://findahelpline.com) are available to connect you to help quickly.

If you're ready to take this beyond the page and into your body, I invite you to experience this principle with me at MillanaSnow.com/ItsAllWithinYou. There you'll find playlists and a guided breathwork practice designed to support your journey. Whether you're reading this in the quiet of your morning or in the thick of a big life decision, come practice with me and let this be the moment you return to your Self.

Integrative Breathwork Practice

Begin by finding a quiet and private place to sit or lie comfortably (lying down flat is ideal). Set a timer or playlist of music of your choosing for fifteen minutes to start. You can work your way up to spend more time with it as you build your practice. Once the timer is set, close your eyes, committing to keeping them closed for the entire length of the timer. Notice how your body feels as it rests on the surface below you, and observe how your everyday breath fills your body.

Begin to listen to the sounds in the environment; instead of ignoring them or trying to make the room silent, invite the sounds in. Treat them as focal points that take you deeper into presence rather than distractions you fight against. This is the perfect metaphor for how we will treat everything in your practice. Everything is for your use, so when you feel something uncomfortable, you can move closer to it rather than push it away. With each breath drawing you deeper into a relationship with whatever comes up, choose a more loving awareness to help you shift into understanding.

As you start to pay attention to sensations around you, you'll move on to some grounding work. This work is key for your body to feel safe and grounded in the present moment. Before you begin the pattern of breath, imagine roots growing from your feet into the ground. Focus on the image until you feel an energetic connection with the roots in your feet and legs. See the roots traveling down into the soil, through the Earth's crust, and into the core. Feel the grounded energy circulating up your legs and spine to reach above the crown of your head, then back down to Earth again. As you notice yourself becoming more present, you'll move on to the breathwork.

Start slowly inhaling through your mouth, directing the breath into your lower belly so it balloons up and out. Then take a second long inhale through your mouth, filling your chest. Lastly, exhale slowly and fully through your mouth, taking time to release all of the breath. Focus on taking long, slow, deep breaths rather than fast, shallow ones. Remind yourself to breathe through the mouth and not the nose: This part is key. Keep this pattern on repeat until the end of the timer or preselected playlist (which is the preferred way of keeping time). Increase the practice time as you get the hang of it, moving through deeper layers of your mind, body, emotions, and spirit with longer practice times.

As you're doing this breathwork, you might start noticing different emotions coming up. The longer your practice, the more opportunities to feel those emotions. As you allow yourself to feel into them, you might ask yourself, "How do I feel?," and let yourself feel the response. Maybe you feel a tingling in your palms, or an ache in your chest. You may get "crab hands" or tetany, where your hand cramps up and clamps inward. If so, slow down, lengthen your exhales, and relax into the body to signal safety. Do your best to focus on the feeling rather than analyzing it, letting your understanding emerge rather than trying to figure it out. Remember: Feel it, to free it, when difficult emotions or bodily sensations emerge. Do your best to stay out of your head and drop your awareness into feeling your body instead. This way, you can use your inhales to move closer to the feelings you're having, and exhales to release them from your system. Know that the feeling of "feeling nothing" is still feeling, too.

When the time is up, come back to your everyday breath and close the practice with a grounding visualization before you open your eyes. Imagine that your body is held by the Earth beneath you; see vines or energy streams gently softening your body into the ground. As you're envisioning this, gently move your fingers and toes. Sway your body from side to side. Then, noting how you feel, slowly open your eyes.

Before rising, if you are lying down, turn to your side into the fetal position. Slowly rise from your side and sit for a moment before getting up. If you're seated, you can simply open your eyes when you're ready. Look around the room and name three colors out loud to ground into your environment. This helps the body remember where it is in the present moment. Drink a few sips of water and begin writing any insights you had in a journal for further reflection and integration.

A few tips for listening to a playlist as a way to guide yourself through different parts of the practice: When I do this, the first ten minutes of the playlist are slow, ambient sounds that help me start feeling the sensations of my body and becoming more present to my mind. In the middle of the practice, the playlist becomes more rhythmic. Then I know it's time to transition to feeling the emotions that are coming up. I find that more emotionally moving music supports my mind to stay with feeling my body and emotions. Then, the playlist slows to softer music and I know it's time to return to normal breathing and slowly exit the practice.

To explore deeper versions of this practice, you're welcome to join me for guided meditations and further training online and in person at MillanaSnow.com/ItsAllWithinYou. There, you'll learn how to safely and compassionately navigate the challenging moments that may come up during longer practices. As you become more comfortable with breathwork, you may enter states of deep reflection or heightened awareness. Throughout this process, remember that you're always in control—you can pause or stop whenever you feel the need. Trust that meaningful inner shifts can happen regardless of how far or deep you go. After your session, support yourself gently: Hydrate well, avoid alcohol and mind-altering substances, and allow yourself quiet time for integration. Consider sharing your experiences selectively with professional guides or trusted friends and family. Regularly practicing presence through breathwork can help you let go of emotional tension, gently question limiting beliefs, and reconnect with your authentic Self. Over time, this intentional presence becomes part of your life, creating room for meaningful change and genuine healing. Everything you seek is already within you. Keep coming back to the breath, and you'll naturally deepen your ability to be present, creating space for transformation and healing.

CHAPTER 4

The Principle of Love

One day when I was about four years old, my grandmother called me into her bedroom for nap time. She told me to lie down, close my eyes, and walk out of my body. Like any well-behaved child, I did just as I was told. I didn't question any of this as she guided me: "See yourself walking around the room. Now float above your body and look down. Go see what your mom is doing in the other room." I was in awe of what I was seeing from my mind's eye. My grandma had me go farther—above the house, where she prompted me to float up more to see all of Denver from a bird's-eye view. Then to float higher to see the whole United States and then the world from space. Without knowing why or ever being told how, I saw every step of the journey just before I drifted to sleep.

From chanting to meditation and visualizations of all types, I spent much of my childhood exploring my inner world. Learning all of this at such a young age gave me the entry point, skill set, and language to come into relationship with the Self long before I even knew what it was called. I came to understand that love is the animating force of everything, and the Self connects us to everything and everyone through love. Love is both a noun and a verb: the unconditional state of being *and* the conscious choice to nurture the growth and flourishing of ourselves and others equally. It seems that we all share a common definition of what love is, but I have a take that may surprise you. It has been over thirty years since I started exploring my inner world, and I have found that at the core of everything, love is who and what we all are.

The Self is love in its purest form. With my clients and in my own healing, my aim is to get in touch with the Self and thereby with the love within. I can't tell you how many times I have sat with clients who were shocked to their core when they came across *real* love in a healing session. When you experience inner love, healing unfolds on its own. When you come into contact with the ineffable qualities of love, it changes you forever. To do this, you have to pull back the layers of resistance to love.

THE CULTURAL MISUNDERSTANDING OF LOVE

In her book *All About Love,* bell hooks laid it bare: "We learn about love in childhood. Whether our homes are happy or troubled, our families functional or dysfunctional, it's the original school of love." Parents might tell their children that their spankings, or some other form of discipline, are "because we love you." As children, we know in our hearts this cannot be true. Something that causes pain surely can't equate to love, but our family and culture demand that we bend the knee to their standard.

This misunderstanding of love isn't limited to individual families; it's deeply ingrained in our culture. In his book *Creating Love* (1992), author John Bradshaw wrote, "I was brought up to believe that love is rooted in blood relationships. You naturally loved anyone in your family. Love was not a choice. The love I learned about was bound by duty and obligation. . . . My family taught me our culture's rules and beliefs about love. . . . [E]ven *with the best intentions* our parents often confused love with what we would now call abuse." For most of us, by the time we are three or four years old, we've all but forgotten what love is.

Love in our society is often based on a transactional exchange of affection, power, obligation, and lust. Love has been exemplified as something that must be earned, and in turn can be lost. Something that one falls in and out of. Something that can be directed discriminately at a person, place, or thing. For many, love is assumed as a built-in fact, merely based on a certain measure of relatedness (family), or of matching characteristics (familiarity). Many people believe that if there was an initial bond of love feelings, love can coexist alongside harm, abuse, and possession. We grow up watching parents cheat and lie, hide and withhold from themselves and each other. We see adults mistreat themselves claiming it's for the love of another. None of this is love. Our cultural definition is the opposite of what love really is, because this, at its best, is conditional affection.

REDEFINING LOVE

Love as a concept is so big and ineffable that words don't suffice. Perhaps that's why its meaning is assumed rather than clearly defined. I aim to define love and loving as a core principle for healing and transformation, as something that you can know and experience for yourself, and *as* yourself. Love is a way of being, as well as an activity of choice. It is the conscious practice of care and nurturance for the growth and well-being of all. It is, as Erich Fromm (1956) says, "the active concern for the life and the growth of that which we love." Love is the animating force, the underlying life principle that facilitates the growth and flourishing of creation. Love is an underlying truth, pervading everyone and everything, the bond among all things and the act of surrendering to it. Love is what some call God—although that definition may complicate things, because our cultural understanding of God is as painfully conditional as our definition of love. Love is attuned. Love is transparent, without agenda or judgment. Love does not harm. Love is not hierarchical and does not exclude. It is creative. All inclusive. Ever expanding. Inherently present. Love encapsulates the very meaning of free will, allowing you freedom to choose its validity or reject its reality.

But most of us are taught that love is based in our relationships with others. This leaves out the fact that the love you have to give emanates from within and is for you to give to yourself first. And it is meant for you to build up within—to then overflow outward to encompass your relationships, your immediate surroundings, and ultimately the entire web of life. The life force of love is in each and every one of us. Love therefore is not what we can give or receive from another person or object, but a state of being that we are and then share (or deny). Love starts within you, because it is the energy that enlivens you. The more you cut it off within yourself, the more you cut off your very aliveness.

THE SELF AS THE SOURCE OF LOVE

Every being is born from love. But not because of your parents. You came into this world as the pure Self, elated to be in your physical form. Innocence is the state of being the unconditional love that you came into this world with. As babies grow, they are taught how this love is allowed to be directed, and with whom. Over time, one moves away from being love, and loving, to exchanging love only when conditions are found appropriate. But the love that is the Self remains. To paraphrase something I once heard Toni Morrison say, "Love is both the thing that holds us all together and the act that continues to bridge the abyss that we imagine separates us." As the life force that animates all things, love is the connective tissue between us. It's the substrate of what makes us all one. The feeling of lacking, of being alone or lonely, is what arises when we lose touch with our innate sense of belonging within the interconnected whole of creation. But all of this is just a spiritual headline if you don't have access to experience this for yourself.

That's where healing comes in. Healing is the process of remembering that you are love and that you can never be separate from it. When you heal, you quickly realize that at your core, you were never alone, you were always enough, and we are all one. And to allow yourself to receive the love that is within is the very foundation for allowing real love to be shared with another. The relationship that we have with love within us will be reflected into the relationships of the external world. No one can reach inside of you and make you receive the love within, because only you can do that. That is why no one can free you or heal you. Only you can choose to know love from the inside out. Thankfully, the forgetting of who and what you are makes the return that much sweeter.

HEALING THROUGH LOVE

One of the most powerful illustrations of what a return to love looks like comes from a client of mine, "Chris," who was looking for support in her love life. She wanted to gain clarity on whether she should divorce her husband. Though she had not yet mentioned any other aspect of her life, I soon found out that there was something much more urgent to explore on the subject of love and relationships. Through breathwork, I guided her into an altered state where I asked her to envision herself sitting at a table in a remote place. I then prompted her to imagine that there were people walking up to the table who she needed to have a conversation with. It could be anyone that came to mind, alive or passed, a total stranger or a well-known family member.

As we went along through each step of the visualization, she and I kept an open dialogue about what she was seeing and feeling. I couldn't see, hear, or feel what was happening within her psyche, so it was important for her to report back so I could help to guide her further. After I gave her the prompt, Chris's face suddenly began to take on a look of utter disgust. Unbeknownst to me, she had experienced incest in her family, a trauma that had been carried out for multiple generations. She was now at the table with the family members who had carried out and enabled these horrendous acts.

The rest she reported play by play: Her daughter was next to her, and her mother was couched between her grandparents, who were sitting behind her. I asked her to speak out loud to whomever she felt called to speak with, to see why they had joined her at the table today. She turned to her grandparents and was able to tell them what she had never been able to say in real life. Defiantly, Chris yelled, "You will never see me or my daughter ever again. You tried to break me but you failed. You knew exactly what you were doing. You're sick. But I made it, and I am not sick like you." She wanted them all to know that she would never allow "such evil" to take the name of love in her life again.

Her face was red, and her body was so hot she was practically steaming. With her rage fuming, she finally had the energy to make a bold departure, with sweat rolling down her face, her hands bunched up as if she was summoning up all her power. But just as she was about to leave and abolish them from her life, and from taking up any more psychic space, she realized that her mother, whom she loved dearly, and who had also been a victim of the abuse, was not leaving with her and her daughter.

Her expression of rage instantly transformed to what looked like abject despair. She begged her mother to leave with her and her daughter, but her mother was despondent. Her mom didn't have the same courage that she did. Despite all the horrible things they had done to her, Chris's mother couldn't leave her parents behind. At this point I could feel a real struggle begin in Chris. And while I had not seen this coming, I knew it was a healing opportunity of a lifetime that I had to support. Despite how intense the emotions had been before, it was clear that Chris was now in an even darker place. She had been here before: Her mother was the reason she hadn't already made a clean break from her abusive family. She had not wanted to leave her mother behind to continue to fall victim to the depravity of the family by herself. By my estimation, this had been the bond that Chris had with her mother, and making a clean break would cut the last thread.

I told Chris to lean into the Self, to let the Self guide her. She had two options before her: to stay in the family to remain with her mom, or to take her daughter far away to create a new definition of love and family. I held firm that this was a choice that only she could make. I guided her to dig deeper with her breath. And after a few seconds, I could see that something was shifting. Perhaps now she was coming into contact with her true Self. Like a bolt of lightning she said, "Real love would not stick around for this." She realized this was true even if that meant leaving her mother behind. In accepting that her mother would not come, Chris did what she always wished her mom had done for her. She took her daughter and left.

As she walked away with her daughter by her side in the visualization, I asked her to check in with herself. "What feeling do you notice in the body?" I asked her, and her face began to shine. With tears in her eyes, she cried, "I feel love. I feel love. Oh my God, *this* is love! I have never felt it like this before. It's almost too much. I'm shaking. *This* is what love is. I've healed this. I've let this go." Chris's whole body was vibrating as if she might explode. In all my years of sessions, I had never seen anyone react this intensely in response to experiencing love. She looked fully enveloped in bliss. It was something so visceral that she almost couldn't move. It was as if she had died and gone to heaven, only now it seemed as though she had also been reborn. As she basked in the process, she shared more of her feelings with me. Leaving her incestuous family behind, she said, also meant that she was clear about something else: that she would be leaving her husband as well. She was complete. She finally understood what real love was, and she knew her life would never be the same. While it would take time to integrate, I knew Chris made a significant change.

Chris's journey speaks to the nature of love and how our understanding of it can be distorted. Let's unpack the lessons we can learn from her experience. In Chris's story you can see how even in the most extreme cases of abuse, someone can be indoctrinated into a family's definition of love. When the love in your family of origin means denying the love that emanates from within, life tends to follow that trend. In Chris's case, it was reconnecting with the love of the Self that gave her the clarity and courage to do what her mother wouldn't. Because genuine love for others stems from Self-love, Chris made a choice that would fortify the love for her daughter rather than the false love of a sick family. That was the moment she understood that her mom and grandparents had that same choice to make for themselves. Perhaps the turning point for Chris was when she surrendered to the real love within her, rather than the codependent delusions of her family of origin. Real love is a choice that every adult has to make for themselves. Only then can harmful generational patterns be broken.

Chris's grandparents were extreme examples of something that happens more than our society would like to admit: that what many people think they understand about love is actually abuse and not love at all. Unfortunately, what Chris and her mom experienced is not uncommon. People stay in harmful family structures out of a sense of obligation or because they honestly believe that this is the only or best kind of love the world has to offer. It occurs all the time. By connecting to the love within, you can see past your family's conditions and illusions.

Until you remember the love that you knew when you came into the world, that ignorance will lead you to seek love from people, objects, or achievements your whole life. And that is a real tragedy. But once you find this love within—and you can—you can free yourself completely. I'm grateful to say that because of true love, I have overcome the greatest traumas imaginable, and many of my clients have done so too. The triumph came from discovering the love that has been there within us the entire time. Chris will likely spend many years integrating and practicing what she learned in that session. Thankfully, the illusion is gone. It will be up to her, the same way it is up to all of us, to keep choosing real love above false representations of it.

Take a moment to breathe. That story may have brought some difficult feelings or memories up for you. Put your hand on your heart and check in. Try breathing through your nose with long, slow breaths. Let yourself be with the feelings and thoughts that Chris's story brought up for you.

CULTIVATING SELF-LOVE

The inner child is just one of those universal parts that has come to believe that it is separate, broken, and in need of something to feel whole again. These parts, or personas, are seeking love and protection from psychic pain. And because they are often totally unconscious factors in your daily life, you might be unaware of your motivations and reasons for making certain decisions about your life. For example, maybe the real reason that you wanted a high-paying, prestigious job where you were the boss was because of a series of humiliating, unresolved events in your childhood. While the details may be more complex than that, I have found that at the end of the day most of our adult struggles arise from parts of ourselves that are seeking love in all the wrong places. Time and time again, I have witnessed people's entire personalities and lives change when they were able to reconnect their inner parts to the love they're seeking from within.

A few years ago, I worked with a woman who was battling cancer. Let's call her "Ivy." Ivy had never done breathwork or inner-parts work but was eager to try. After years of dealing with mental illness and now stage four cancer, she was hungry for healing. Despite her history of being institutionalized, Ivy trusted me to help her explore her inner world, warning me that it might go haywire. As I guided her inward, asking what she saw, she described a vast expanse of desert and scorched earth, filled with what she called "crazy people." She witnessed starving children and desperate vagrants ready to attack at any moment. It was a scary hellscape, and she wanted to get out fast.

Unfortunately, years of neglecting trauma can do that. Together we understood that it was the dread of her inner realm and absence from it that had turned her once verdant oasis into a desolate underworld. If we could stay to cultivate what was ready to heal and be transformed, Ivy's inner world and all its languishing parts would be much better off. Thankfully, Ivy was willing to trust that if we continued on, with courage, compassion, and unconditional love, there would be a great reward. This is what choosing love looks like—even if you don't like what you see. Sometimes when you look, things appear bleak, but this is where and when love is needed the most.

As we continued the meditation, I asked Ivy to identify who in this desert landscape needed the most urgent support. She described a younger version of herself. Her inner child was emaciated, desperate for love and attention. As we approached younger Ivy, it was clear that this child was terrified. I guided Ivy to speak to her younger self, expressing interest in helping her heal. We invited the inner child to speak out loud through Ivy, so that I could hear the conversation as well. Her inner child—let's call her "Fergie"—suddenly came to life, and Ivy's physical body visibly changed before my eyes. Ivy's adult body became twisted and small, her face downtrodden yet innocent. She spoke with a timid voice, carrying an air of irritation and distrust. I introduced myself to Fergie, explaining that her older self had sought my help for healing. I assured her of my intentions to help her be heard and get the love and support she needed.

After some convincing, Fergie opened up. She shared her experiences of abuse, of being left to fend for herself without the protection and love of safe adults. She expressed her distrust of her older self, who had also neglected and mistreated her over the years. Fergie cried out with loud sobs, exhausted and hurt. It was clear she was barely holding on. Remembering my client's medical condition, I couldn't help but wonder if Fergie's pain had some impact on the state of Ivy's physical health.

I gently guided Ivy to feel the energy of her Self while encouraging utmost honesty as she shared her thoughts and feelings with Fergie. Perhaps from the perspective of love and nonattachment, Ivy could make some headway with Fergie. Ivy wailed for some time before finally speaking to her younger self. "You're right," she said. "I have neglected you. I have left you to deal with the most horrible pain all by yourself. And you're right, I have abused you and let others do the same. I am so, so sorry." Although I could see that it was painful, this was also clearly incredibly healing for Ivy, and for her inner child too. The love and honesty was beautiful to witness.

Watching this unfold reminded me that we all came into this world knowing how to love, because love is who we are. But with so much that goes on in our childhoods, we were conditioned and trained away from our truth. As children, we learned to withhold, manipulate, judge, and distrust to survive. Ivy reminded me that, when we're supported to reengage our inherent traits of discernment, kindness, and compassion, they're immediately available, even if they have been long ignored. Somehow, almost like magic, real love and compassion appear, as if they were there and waiting for us to allow them in.

After some time, I spoke to Fergie, asking if she had heard her older self. Was Fergie willing to rebuild trust? Fergie admitted that, although she believed that her adult self was sincere and open to rebuilding trust between them, she felt that her older self would need to prove that she meant it this time. We discussed the importance of their connection—their destinies were tied as long as they shared this body. Fergie understood this and expressed her need for care and attention to be nursed back to health. Ivy agreed, already feeling a deep sense of release within her mind, emotions, and body. She reported that a lightness of being overcame her that she hadn't felt in a long time. Ivy was clear and committed to showing up in a new way.

Ivy came back for another session a few months later and announced that she was cancer free. I couldn't say how such a miracle happened, and I want to be clear that I am not saying this came from our session. I believe that the inner work she was doing helped. It's important for me to reiterate that this healing work is not a replacement for medical treatment. In fact, Ivy was not only making changes to her lifestyle and diet at the time but was also doing cancer treatments with her oncologists that were working. This healing work is complementary to medical intervention. Inner healing helps you win the battles of life, whatever those may be—whether that is fighting cancer or facing death. As James Baldwin (1962) once said, "Not everything that can be faced can be changed, but nothing can be changed that is not faced."

This is what love looks like in action: You tend to the garden of your inner world, because no one can do that for you. Ivy's session was only ninety minutes, but it was like decades of talk therapy in one sitting. Mere seconds of just showing up for yourself, let alone really loving yourself even when it's hard, can help heal and transform even the direst of circumstances.

Sadly, most people not only don't know this is possible but will do everything they can to avoid facing themselves when their pain starts to surface. And I get it, it can be scary sometimes. But this kind of inner exploration is not about getting a result or even being cured. You are more than a body, you are a whole person that needs love to thrive regardless of what the outcome looks like.

The principle of love is most important when you don't want to love yourself. It's when you're most sick of yourself that you need *your* love the most. Like a garden that's overrun by weeds or parasites, your mind and body need attention, recognition, and care when they are racked with anxiety, fear, illness, and confusion. Self-hatred and self-judgment turn your back on what is yours to cultivate. In loving yourself, you must turn toward yourself and accept who and what you find, so that you can love it back into wholeness. And it doesn't have to be "work" all the time either. Just like in gardening, you get to have fun too.

Love is accepting and without agenda. When you accept what is, you make space for what can be. This is how you transform yourself. But often, we deny who we've become, how we feel, or how life is unfolding. You might deny your reality for so long that you end up completely neglecting yourself, making your situation even more toxic. When things have run amok in your life, it's likely that denial and neglect have been playing out unconsciously for a long time. What in your life have you been in denial about? What truths about yourself have you been rejecting? Not just the "ugly" stuff: The beautiful truths can be rejected as well.

Now is the time to come back into relationship with your Self and really ask. Relationship, even within yourself, requires connection, acceptance, and nurturance. Simply put, this means treating yourself better. Rather than punishing yourself, which many people are taught to do when they "mess up," you must care for yourself with the love and kindness you would offer an innocent child. You can start to reconnect to the Self within you by simply having an open and honest conversation. Let yourself check in, see what comes to mind, and see if you accept where you are. So you can start to build a healthier relationship with all the parts of you that feel disconnected.

As you practice accepting yourself as the Self does, you might notice how you feel the relief of no longer fighting against what is true. Acceptance is about "being with" rather than rejecting. Imagine your younger self on your worst day, sitting on a riverbank. Now see your adult self, walking over and sitting next to the younger you without saying anything. Just let your loving presence be enough to let the younger you know that they are loved and not alone. This is what "being with" yourself is like. It's showing up for you as the loving presence that you need. When you begin to show up for you, as Ivy and Chris did, all your other relationships have a real chance to be the soul connections you've dreamt of. Because now you know how to show up the way real love does. Now you are embodied love, no longer acting out the false beliefs of what love isn't.

At the end of this chapter, I'll share some of the same practices that I shared with Chris and Ivy so that you can try it out for yourself. While I could list a million tips about how to find and keep a great relationship, all the love and relationship advice in the world pales in comparison to what is possible when you find love within yourself. Because when you love yourself, amazing relationships will follow. The love that you allow yourself to experience within is the love that you will experience in the world. I can promise you that.

LOVE VERSUS ATTACHMENT

Perhaps the reason that loving ourselves is so challenging is that so many of us have never known unconditional love from another human. Love in our society and in our families is often more like attachment. When you become attached, you become a barrier to love. Vedanta scholar and philosopher A. Parthasarathy (2014) states it plainly: "Love and attachment are opposed to each other. Attachment is perversion of love." We become attached to people and things because we believe they are what will make us happy and whole. But you are already whole. And *you* are where the feelings of love come from. This is what the sages have been trying to remind us, but our society doesn't listen. Love in the external world is a reflection of the love within you. Seeking love, belonging, and wholeness in another is like expecting your reflection in the mirror to smile before you do. Despite what most of us are taught, attachment to people, places, and things will eventually cause suffering.

Who and what you will love will pass. Your body, personality, and belongings are passing. Attachment to anything is attachment to suffering. And because real love has no agenda, it is only found in the present moment. Free from limitation, love is unattached because its very nature is that of growth and change. And because love is the animating force of all things, loss and separation are the illusions of our humanness rather than the reality. Love transforms us again and again, beyond what we recognize as ourselves. And because love will eventually have its way, it's so much easier to let go and let love do its thing. Let go of suffering (resistance to love) rather than being attached to the ephemeral (fear).

It is critical to relearn how to live and love this way. Otherwise, you'll live your life thinking that someone is going to save you, make you feel whole, or finally give you the love you deserve. I've seen clients who took jobs they hated so that their parents would accept them, only to find that when they did finally get that prestigious title, they still felt devoid of the love they were seeking. I have worked with others who practice self-love as a core principle for living and have completely resolved the pain of their abusive and neglectful parents, going on to become the first in their family to marry their soulmate. I invite you to practice the exercises that follow so that you can begin to live as you once did as a child who knew true love. And if you cannot remember such a time, now is the time to begin again. So that you can see yourself and the world as the Self does. As you begin to reacquaint yourself with the real love within, you will find that all the guidance and clarity you needed on love in your relationships will be abundantly available to you. Like all the core principles of healing and transformation, this practice may gently return you to your Self, where your inherent wisdom, joy, and worth already reside.

Practicing Love

- Create a private space so that you can explore your feelings and be uninhibited.
- Take your time, listen to your body.
- Stay hydrated and nourished, as even the simplest practices can use a profound amount of energy.
- Ground yourself before and after each exercise to set the tone and create safety. This could mean setting intentions, journaling, and making a sacred space.
- Do your best to stay off of devices and avoid outside distractions by silencing or turning off your phone.
- Lastly, if you ever feel overwhelmed by emotions, memories, or physical sensations, contact a trauma-informed mental health professional. If ever in an emergency, call 911 or find an available helpline at https://findahelpline.com.

Meet Your Self

Read the following instructions all the way through before you begin, and then guide yourself in following them.

Begin by setting a timer for fifteen minutes. This might sound quite long, but trust me, it goes by very fast.

Next, choose a comfortable position. When you're comfortable, close your eyes. Then, lying flat, begin with breathwork. Breathe in through your mouth into your lower belly, letting your belly balloon up and out. Take a second to inhale through the mouth again, expanding your chest. Then exhale it all out through the mouth with a slow and long release. Repeat through the timer.

As you breathe, notice the sounds that you hear in your current environment, letting go of your need to change or silence them. As you continue to breathe, feel your body on the surface below you. How does your body feel? Are you tense in the shoulders? Tightening your belly? Perhaps you start to notice your thoughts. Just as with the sounds that you hear externally, allow your thoughts to pass without judgment or intervention. Just notice them. As you are changing your physiological state with the pattern of your breath, you may notice a shift in your emotions. Allow these emotions to come up, breathing into the feelings that come up in your body. When you notice that you feel present and accepting of your thoughts and emotions, you can begin the visualization.

Imagine yourself alone in a dark room. As you breathe, begin to deepen your sense of what it feels like to be in this space alone. Treat your breath like footsteps that help you reach deeper into the void. Spend some time feeling for your higher Self. What does your inner guidance look like? Can you see it? Can you reach for it somewhere? Do you sense its presence? As you continue to breathe, notice your thoughts and let them pass through, like they're slipping between your fingers, as you continue to feel for your higher Self.

Continuing to breathe, you might call out to your inner world. Call to the Self like you would a lost loved one. "Where are you? Do you hear me?" Keep going. Do not give up. You might start to feel a warmth or a sense of someone familiar in your vicinity. Keep breathing the pattern of breath, allowing yourself to lean toward the warmth or whatever starts to appear. As you start to move into a feeling of love and acceptance, reach toward it, as if feeling for a light switch in the dark. Begin to perceive what your true Self looks like. You might even say, "What do you look like?" or "Please show me." Meanwhile, continue to breathe: two slow inhales, in through the mouth, one long exhale out through the mouth.

Finally, ask the Self for the message that you most need to receive now. What does your inner wisdom want you to know? Once you have your answer, believe what you received and thank your Self for guiding you today. Take a moment to feel each inhale and exhale.

Come back to your everyday breath after the timer or playlist is finished. Then wiggle your fingers and toes and become aware of your surroundings again. Take a few deep breaths in and out and open your eyes when you're ready. Ground yourself by calling out three colors that you see in the room. Journal or voice-record any of your learnings and reflections.

Repeat this process and practice it as much as needed, extending the time as long as you like. If you didn't find your Self or notice the Self's presence, that's okay. Not everyone does at first. Just keep coming back to this and I promise that your Self will find you.

CHAPTER 5

The Principle of Integration

INTEGRATION IS LIKE WEAVING AN UNRAVELED BASKET BACK together. The more you integrate the threads of yourself back into wholeness, the more of your life you can carry and draw from. By integrating your life's experiences, you tie off the loose ends of the past, expanding your capacity to hold life's joys and challenges, growing stronger and more fulfilled along the way. Without integration, life weighs you down, because you keep trying to carry all the fragments of yourself that remain stuck in a painful past. When you carry all of these pieces of yourself from the past, they can become so heavy that you can barely stand the burden.

No matter what your history may be, living in this world requires that you carry some burdens along the way. But you were meant to put those burdens down eventually. Over time, if they remain unintegrated, it's likely that you have come to let those burdens define you instead. Perhaps, unconsciously, you forgot that life isn't what you've been through, but what you did with it all. Integration is the tool that helps you make use of what life has brought you so that you can transform your past experiences into wisdom and creative power.

When you learn the principle of integration, you learn how to see your life in terms of wholeness. As you begin to see yourself from this higher perspective, you can begin to shift your beliefs from limitation to abundance. Through this lens, you'll be able to make healthier choices and accept more empowering ways of living. In this framework of healing, we aim to bring everything into awareness to integrate it back into the Self. The word "heal" comes from the Old English word *hælan*, "to make whole, sound, or well." The root of the word *hælan*, in turn, is the Proto-Indo-European *kailo* or *kailos*, "whole" or "uninjured." This so perfectly illustrates what integration is about. When you integrate, you heal by merging with the original uninjured Self within. And with a little inner exploration and a drop of loving acceptance, you'll reclaim the wholeness that lies at the heart of you, allowing you to chart a new life of your choosing. The practices and stories ahead offer you the opportunity to merge with your original, uninjured Self, and all it takes to begin is just a little bit of your attention and care.

FROM FRAGMENTATION TO WHOLENESS: WHY WE ALL NEED INTEGRATION

A few years ago, after reading an article in *New York* magazine, I checked out a woman's YouTube channel that it had featured.

She was one of the first YouTubers to openly share what it was like to have dissociative identity disorder (DID), previously known as multiple personality disorder. DID is a coping mechanism that typically emerges when a child has experienced severe and prolonged trauma. To deal with the trauma, the brain blocks out memories and creates entire personalities in order to disassociate. These "alters," as she called them, or "parts," as they're called in the IFS therapy model, develop different memories and have their own preferences and needs. They are all separate from the "host," who is the main personality that leads the body and the system of alters.

These parts all have roles (both conscious and unconscious) that help regulate the system and keep the body safe. For example, the DID YouTuber had a grandmother-like inner part whose job it was to help keep the system and body calm. While watching her parts "come out" on camera, it occurred to me that while most of us don't suffer from DID, we all have parts that live within us, fighting to get their needs met. Somewhat like her identities, our parts are seeking expression and self-preservation. At their core, they're desperately searching for resolution. Because they didn't get a chance to reconcile the trauma that occurred at the time they emerged, these parts broke off, believing there was no way they were going to survive if they didn't.

This is also why the trauma of separating from our core Self can come about even when "good" things occur, too—like, for example, when a young man has discovered that he has fallen in love with another man but denies the bliss of romantic love, so that he can be a "good son" to his parents, who only consider a good son to be a straight man. In this example, the repressed inner part breaks off and the "good son" persona hardens and mutates into a painful protective mask, leaving the young man split between two worlds that he can never fully enjoy. We have all felt torn like this, and integration is how we bridge the gap.

When working with the principle of integration, it's less about what happens to us than about the meaning we make of what happened. Over a lifetime, integration becomes a vital tool, not only for healing trauma but for maturing and growing into fuller versions of ourselves. Integration helps us to continue to reclaim ourselves and to live more authentic and resilient lives. At its core, it is the work and the fun that goes along with maturing. By consciously weaving our parts and experiences back into the whole Self, we free ourselves from our limiting beliefs and open ourselves up to our full potential. In the process, we consciously choose the meaning of the events of our lives and thereby how we respond to them. In calling yourself back through integration, you'll discover parts of yourself that you didn't know existed, and you'll remember things that you didn't know you forgot. By the end of this chapter, you'll have both the practices and the context to do just that.

Take a moment to breathe. Is there a part of you that wants your attention? Does this part have a name? An age? A message?

INTEGRATING MY FRAGMENTED PARTS: BIG SIS

I want to share a personal story about how I was able to learn about integration firsthand. When I was around nineteen years old, I unconsciously had a split in my overall personality. Looking back, I understand that a new part "came to the front," meaning that this part was the new host and dominant personality of Millana. I went from being a shy and bookish girl to an arrogant and fierce teenager. This new persona appeared organically, whereas in the past, due to constantly moving while growing up, I had consciously architected my personality to fit in. In my late teens, with continuous bullying at school and daily psychological abuse at home, I needed a strong disposition that would help me rise above shame and humiliation. Enter "Big Sis," a protective part of me who emerged as a self-described "bad bitch" that "didn't give a fuck." Yes, those were her exact words.

Big Sis veiled herself under the cover of Millana for years, but she first emerged to protect and ready me for early adulthood. She made sure I was able to deal with all the aggression that came my way. She was tough, she got what she wanted, and she was clear that she would no longer tolerate disrespect. Unbeknownst to me at the time, Big Sis was how I started modeling, moved to New York, and created powerful new alliances that put me in a position to rise above my station. I much preferred life like this and forgot I had ever been any other way.

I didn't know this was just one part of myself and not my whole personality until years later, when Big Sis started to come into conflict with a new part that emerged in my late twenties. I was ready for a meaningful relationship, and this "bad bitch" was not interested. Big Sis wanted powerful men to bend the knee to her. She only wanted to be in nonsexual relationships where she was emotionally safe and financially propped up. Because the ego personality of Big Sis was so strong, I reveled in the loyalty and protection of powerful older men despite the incongruence between these relationships and my spiritual calling. In the years that followed, Big Sis and my other parts began to go to war, which self-sabotaged my dating life in ways that felt completely out of my control. Sometimes, I would meet a great guy, and just as things were getting serious, I would lash out and push him away in the most dramatic way possible. Had I understood the power of the principle of integration earlier, I would have had a much easier time creating healthy relationships.

But because I didn't know how to integrate this part of myself, I shut her down. In an effort to find more meaningful relationships, I exiled Big Sis deep into my inner world. Now, instead of seeking out powerful men to soothe my deep-seated need for protection and power, I sought out men who were kind but just as afraid of the world as I was. I got myself into serious relationships that quickly moved into disempowering situations that left us both scrounging for the world's leftovers. Now that Big Sis wasn't allowed, I lacked the grit and confidence to go for what I needed to survive. I had more intimacy and meaning, but I was struggling with men whose main goal was just to get by. It wasn't until my late twenties that I realized that I had to bring these parts of myself into harmony. And it wasn't until my mid-thirties that I learned who Big Sis was by name.

One day, while I was journaling with my inner child, I felt the presence of a part that was ready to speak. It was as if someone was trying to get my attention, but from within me. From doing parts work with my inner child, I knew it was important to get curious, to open up to this part and ask who it was. She told me her name was Big Sis. I asked her how old she was (a way for understanding the time that the part split off), and I heard, "Aw, I'm somewhere between nineteen and twenty-one." As with anytime you meet a new person, it's important to ask questions and listen to get to know them. So, I did, and she started to tell me what she thought about the situation I was journaling about. She expressed herself with a surprising amount of arrogance. I felt a jolt of cavalier pride as I let her come through. She was sassy, biting in her honesty, and incredibly clear on who she was. It felt electrifying. But her attitude was also tinged with negativity.

Because of the work I'd done with my clients, I knew to pick up on the subtleties of her personality while letting her speak and air out her feelings without judgment. She wanted me to understand that "no one gets to treat us with disrespect," and that if we were going to "make it big in this life, we better let them know who we are." After a few minutes, I realized that I knew Big Sis well. I just never knew her by name. I remembered she had been me for years, protecting me so that I never felt as lowly as I once had as a young girl. After listening until she was done, I told her I appreciated her and wanted to learn her ways. But at this stage of my life, her beliefs about relationships would need some updating, as it seemed that she was working under the assumption that everyone around me was trying to hurt me.

She acknowledged that her anger and pride weren't helpful when individuals who treated me with kindness and unconditional love were the only people around. We understood that I needed Big Sis to protect me when I was too young to move away from my family or take care of myself. Like all of our parts, Big Sis just wanted the best for me. She had once helped me create a better life for myself. Now she was here to remind me to have the confidence to believe that I deserved to be treated with respect and kindness. Even now, she wanted the best for me, and she understood pretty quickly that maybe not everything about her way of looking at things was helpful.

I journaled and spoke with Big Sis daily for a period of a few months. She was funny, assertive, and as energizing as can be. Connecting with this part helped me learn so much about myself. Then, one day, while journaling with Big Sis, she had an announcement.

She was ready to integrate with the Self. She expressed to me that, at first, she had resisted this idea. In many ways, merging with the Self felt like dying; her singular identity would dissolve, and she feared she would cease to exist. At the same time, she understood that the role she played was no longer needed.

All of a sudden I felt a heavy, foreboding feeling that I could only describe as death. "Am I dying?" I asked, as I called on the Self to help navigate what was coming up. The Self explained that the feeling of death that was looming was simply the feeling of fear. If I was willing to let the fear go, we'd see that Big Sis's return would yield more life. The Self explained that Big Sis would now have all the resources and possibilities of the eternal Self, rather than just the limited stories of a finite past burdened by pain. If Big Sis was willing to return to wholeness, this would help me and the whole system of my parts to access all of Big Sis's assertiveness and clear-minded discernment, rather than the burden that came with her survival-based agenda.

Then, the next day, without notice, I felt that she had passed through and into the Self. Into me. While it's hard to express what that feels like, what I can say is that I felt more like myself. I felt more rooted in my worthiness. I felt safer and better able to speak both my boundaries and affections. I now know I deserve to be treated with kindness and care, and how to act with integrity in holding to that standard. In the past, I put up with a lot because I thought I had to prove I was worthy of being treated with respect and kindness. Now, I know I don't need to beg or prove myself. I know that kindness is an inalienable right. It took days to get used to how this new way of seeing things felt in my body. I suppose it's the calm feeling that comes with grounded inner confidence. These were just a few of the many gifts that came from integrating Big Sis. And while I don't feel her taking over anymore, I still sense her.

THE PARTS THAT ARE READY TO INTEGRATE IN YOU

Who's your Big Sis? The protective part that rises up to defend you? As you read this, you may be starting to get a sense. Often, when speaking with clients about the subject of integrating parts, they report having flashbacks or tingling sensations, feeling anxious, or experiencing fluctuations in their body temperature. Your inner world is so connected that your parts can hear what you're thinking and feeling, even what you are reading about. If you tune in, you'll notice that you can feel and hear them, too. Bodily sensations, tingles, and tears are the first signs.

What do you notice in your body right now? What thoughts do you hear? Thoughts are parts speaking to each other. Listen to your thoughts long enough, and you'll find out who's talking. You'll find this out by making space for integration through listening, reflecting, and feeling. But you can simply ask too. Perhaps it's more obvious that we need integration when something significant in our lives happens. Newlywed couples often report wishing they'd had a few more days or a longer honeymoon before jumping right back into life. Intuitively, they understand they need time and space to settle in to a new identity, even if they have lived together for years. Integration is about acknowledging the new roles that you have taken on and giving them the room to harmonize.

Sometimes, integration is called for when small changes have accumulated and a new desire presents itself. A new desire could be as small as how wonderful it would be to draw every day. In listening and reflecting, you might realize that this small action is how you're beginning to reclaim your capacity for creative expression. To integrate, for example, could be as small as allowing yourself to see yourself as someone who draws or paints. Drawing every day might lead you to new interests and opportunities. At the very least, you'll cultivate more joy. Perhaps, in time, you'll reclaim your inner artist. At the end of this chapter, we will explore practices that will help you integrate your thoughts, feelings, parts, and experiences so you can draw from their medicine. In the process, you'll start to feel more like yourself again. Centered, confident, calm, and much more joyful.

Integration isn't just about what happens when you work with your parts; it's also what happens in the brain, mind, and body when you change how you look at things. Sometimes, integration can take days, weeks, or even years. But sometimes, when done with deep, uninterrupted presence, how you look at reality can change in seconds. While it might take time for the changes you have made to sort themselves out in your life, the change of mind can happen quickly.

This happened to me recently. It was a day that would change the rest of my life. I was in Northern California on vacation. It was just a couple of days after the Fourth of July, and I had taken the afternoon to catch up on a few work calls. I was tired and ready to return to the holiday activities when my then boyfriend approached me outside. He turned to me with a serious look and said, "I can't wait any longer!" Confused, I asked him what he meant as I noticed him beginning to bend down and reach into his pocket. "Will you marry me, Millana?" he asked. Totally shocked by the timing, I checked in with myself before answering what I long rehearsed to myself. "Yes, yes, yes," I heard in every layer of my inner being. "Yes!" I said out loud.

It was a euphoric moment. Just the two of us, at one of our favorite places in the world. I was basking in the love and excitement for a few minutes, when suddenly, sadness began to creep into my awareness. I tried to busy myself with telling family and friends so I could ignore what I feared was doubt. Had I missed something? Was there something or someone within me that didn't want this? I dreaded the thought, and the feelings became heavier and heavier by the minute. I knew this was a life-changing moment and that I needed to integrate whatever came up. I asked my new fiancé to give me a few minutes while I checked in with myself. I went straight into journaling, asking, at the top of the page, "Who is feeling sad right now?" There was an immediate response: "It's me, the girlfriend. The woman you just were but will never be again." I felt the grief and longing in my heart as I continued writing. "I was the girlfriend, living this way for years. There was always a back door. I could leave if I wanted. But now, there is no back door. And I went from living in the world to being pushed inside instantly."

I was shocked, but it all rang true. Looking back, I realized that my new fiancé had had months of preparation. When he had bought the ring, months ago, he had already integrated this new role within himself. Although we had spoken about getting married many times, it had never occurred to me that saying yes also meant letting go of a part of myself. In taking this step forward, I became a woman I had not yet known. I was no longer the girlfriend who had an exit plan. I was a woman who was ready for a lifelong commitment. Can you imagine how my now inner girlfriend part would have acted out had I not listened to her?

I've seen it with clients many times. Now I finally understood it for myself. When we leave parts of ourselves out of the maturation process, cheating, lying, and hiding from the next step in adulthood is inevitable. Sometimes, listening is all that's needed to integrate. In honoring this stage in my life, I was able to lovingly bring my girlfriend story to a close. I was able to thank the girlfriend and honor that part of myself. As I let myself be with this part of me, I felt closure. There were no more loose ends. She was complete now. The sadness turned to pure joy and gratitude for the full life that I have lived and the fuller life that had just begun.

I have had many clients in the past who were too afraid to listen to that small voice that whispered that something was off. I have also had clients who were too afraid to listen to others—even when their partner told them point blank that they didn't want to get married. It's understandable for someone to be afraid to listen to those small inner voices, but to reject the truth is to deny a part of yourself. When we don't listen to our inner voices, we have a hard time honoring another's inner truth. When we refuse integration, those parts do all kinds of things to get our attention. Cheating, overworking, self-harming, or striking out in fits of anger are all symptoms of ignoring that voice that needs your attention.

Sometimes, you realize the reality that a relationship is over. Often, what's really going on is much deeper than what your fears would have you believe. Sometimes your inner voice just needs to be heard, and no action is required. I've seen clients on the brink of cheating realize that their issue was an inner teenager who hadn't gotten over a high school heartbreak. Instead of something being "wrong" in their current relationship, they just needed to integrate their younger parts so they could show up maturely and get new results. Integration is about breaking free of the web of stories that have shrouded you in fear, guilt, and shame. And when you do, your body also shifts, because it's no longer holding the weight of those long-held emotions. Your overall mood changes when you no longer feel you are missing something. And when you make it a lifestyle, your whole life gets better and better.

THE PROCESS OF INTEGRATION

When you consciously integrate, your personality becomes more productive and healthy. This is what maturity is really about. Maturation isn't about aging, but the completion of a phase of life that is no longer being lived in the external world. I'm sure you can think of someone in their late sixties or even seventies who has the emotional maturity of a teenager. It's almost as if their personality stopped evolving with their body and life experiences. This is an example of how maturity has nothing to do with one's age or societal position, but is instead an attunement to the cycles of life. My teacher, Dr. Clara Mosely, is in her eighties, and her youthful energy burns just as brightly as her hard-won wisdom. She is a well-integrated woman who has consciously worked with and completed the many cycles of her life. And because of that, she's more alive than most thirty-somethings I know. She walks around as if every cell of her body is as free as it wants to be.

Integration is an alchemical process of freeing you up for more aliveness. What you integrate becomes nutritive. What you transform and release becomes a gift to others. Permit yourself to encircle the trauma of your past experiences with awareness and love for even a moment uninterrupted, and you'll transform those traumatic events into historical facts, leaving you with profound understanding and empathy. I know this to be true because this book is a product of my own alchemical process. It might sound ridiculous to imagine that you can resolve the most horrific traumas within yourself. Some think this gives credit to the people who caused the harm. That's not the case. These principles are grounded in the understanding that resolution comes from getting to the root of what happened *inside* you rather than what happened *to* you. We cannot always control what happens to us, but through integration, we make it possible to resolve it all within ourselves. In the following exercises, you'll discover precisely how to do that. You can do them now, or save them for when you have about an hour to give it your full attention.

Practicing Integration

It's important to check in with yourself to ensure that this practice is right for you at this time. While these practices are self-led, they can bring about intense emotions and painful memories and might be best explored with an IFS professional or a trauma-informed professional trained in parts work. If you have complex trauma, I highly recommend working with a professional when doing these exercises. You can find certified IFS practitioners at the IFS Institute's Practitioner Directory (https://ifs-institute.com/practitioners). If you are currently in a crisis or feel emotionally overwhelmed, please reach out to a helpline or mental health support service for immediate assistance. Resources like Find a Helpline (https://findahelpline.com) are available to connect you to help quickly.

Parts Journaling

Create a private space where you can move, emote, and make the faces, expressions, sounds, and shapes that you want to make freely. Close the door and the blinds and let those in close proximity know that you will need privacy for the full amount of time the door is closed. Dress in comfortable clothes. Have water nearby, and use the restroom before you begin so you can do the session uninterrupted. Use a physical journal with a pen or pencil. I've found that this practice is more impactful when you do it this way rather than making notes in your phone. Light a candle or incense to set a meaningful tone for the practice. Set a timer for at least thirty minutes. You'll want to write for the bare minimum of that time. But no longer than an hour to start.

To begin, do a grounding practice. Grounding is key for your body and parts to feel safe in the present moment. You can imagine roots coming from your feet and into the ground. Take a few moments to do this until you feel centered in your body.

Set an intention and open your heart and mind. For example, "I welcome any parts of myself that need to come forward." While there may be a few parts that come up during the exercise, it will be key to deal with them one at a time. Take your time and pause as you need to. Do your best to stay in the practice for the full length of time on the timer. I recommend that you not do this practice for over an hour at a time, to avoid overthinking. Feel free to break the exercise up into multiple sessions as needed. You can also work with one part at a time over the course of a month so as not to overwhelm yourself.

Often, protector parts will arise first, in order to shield you and your more vulnerable parts from feeling difficult emotions. These parts may try to distract you or push you away, and that's okay. Do your best to accept and acknowledge each part as it comes. If there is frustration or irritation, speak with the part that is irritated first. Remember, every part is doing the best it can to protect you and help you get your needs met. Honor the experience of the parts and work with them to go deeper in their own time. When things feel challenging or stuck, you can call your Self forward to support you in your inner world. Sometimes just being with these parts is enough. Don't push, and do your best to remain open, loving, and patient whenever there is resistance to moving forward.

Make Initial Contact

Begin by writing a greeting and sharing your intention in your journal. Keep it as real, honest, and transparent as possible. As you start writing, remember that you will not stop until the timer goes off. This will be a nonstop writing practice. Even if it's babble or you don't know what to say, you want to keep the pen moving. You can write, "I don't know what to say." Literally write whatever comes out. Logic need not apply. Trust the process and allow yourself to go wherever the pen takes you.

For example, it might start something like, "Hello, I get the sense that there is a part of me that is sad about this new job that I have begun this week. I feel that you have been trying to get my attention. I would like to speak with you about this so that I can get to know you and understand how you feel." Part: "Yes, I hate this job. We were never supposed to do work like this. You broke your promise to me . . ."

Get to Know Them

As you allow whatever comes out on the page to continue, feel the emotions that come forward in the process. You might also start to have memories as you hear from parts. Allow yourself to acknowledge these memories with your parts as if you just saw a scene play out together. As a part begins to speak, get to know it a bit better. Listen without judgment, and thank your part for coming forward and doing its best. Let your parts know that they don't have to share everything in one session. Continue to get to know them like you would a new neighbor or friend. This might look like, "Thank you for showing up and speaking. What is your name? How old are you? What else would you like me to know about what you are like and what you are feeling?"

Build Understanding

Do your best to really connect with and understand the parts that present themselves. If they are shy or protective, feel free to ask them about that so you can understand how to help them feel more at ease. Let them express themselves and their needs and concerns. Get to know their roles and reasons for being. Ask them why and how they emerged. Notice any bodily shifts or emotions that arise, and feel them as you communicate. Take your time and do your best to listen to and feel what each part is sharing with you. Attune to them. Listen and allow them to express themselves.

This might look like, "Thank you for letting me know more about you. Could you tell me more about why you emerged at eleven years old? What is your purpose and what do you feel you need most? What is one thing you wished I understood about you? If you could change one thing about the way I responded to you, what would it be? How can I support you right now?"

Help Release Stress or Pain

Once you have spent some time connecting with a part, ask it what it needs to release some of its stress or pain. If you are speaking with a protective part or a part that is still uneasy about feelings, ask what you can do to help it to feel safe enough to let go of what it has been carrying. At this point, regardless of the time on your timer, allow yourself to stop writing so that you can feel and release emotions in real time. You may cry or have other forms of physical release. Let it happen. Before closing, ask your part if there is anything it needs from you to unburden.

Close the Session

Be sure to make time at the end of the exercise to reflect on what you just experienced with your parts. Stay away from your phone or other distractions until you have formally closed the session. Check in: How do you feel? What does your body feel like now? Do you notice any changes in the way you see things? Note any changes or insights in your journal for future reference. Be sure to acknowledge yourself, both your body and your parts, for showing up today.

Make a plan for next steps. Following up with your agreements moving forward is of the utmost importance. Make a plan for how you will keep the commitments that came up in the session. Actively make space for the part you encountered to have a healthy and joyful place in your life. Make a date to meet again within a week, and repeat this practice at that time. It's important to keep contact, as this is how you build a healthy ecosystem of parts that feel safe enough to share their wisdom and needs.

Take time for grounding again while you close the container of this practice. Breathe deeply and slowly in through your nose down to your belly and slowly out through your mouth. Feel your feet on the ground and gently pat your legs in an alternating pattern. Say three colors that you see out loud and touch five objects, making sure to really feel the textures and temperatures. Clean up your space and close your journal while saying thank you to your parts and to your higher Self. Open your calendar and put the next date down as a meeting that you plan to keep.

CHAPTER 6

The Principle of Grief

GRIEF IS ONE OF THE MOST FEARED AND MISUNDERSTOOD PRINciples of the seven I'll be presenting. Most people think of it as a scary pain they'll one day have to endure. It's no wonder we avoid it, as it's often only considered when we're mourning the loss of someone we love. And while there are many resources that offer guidance on grief as it relates to death, few speak to how grief can be used as a tool for spiritual growth and personal transformation. Grief, from this perspective, is a vehicle that can help you detach from what is no longer working, thriving, serving, or "alive" to embody what is. Grief is a mechanism that allows you to let go of the past so you can open to what is available now, whether it's a new perspective, a new habit, or a new stage of life. That is why it's so vital to know how to work with grief. Without it, you can stay stuck in the past. In fact, when you feel stuck in life, it may be a red flag that you've gotten stuck in the grieving process.

Working with grief from this vantage point can support you in your everyday life. For example, say you feel stuck in your job. No matter how hard you try to prove yourself, you can't seem to catch a break. Despite all the hard work, you feel unable to proceed to the next stage of your career. When you drive to work, you know something isn't right, but you plow through, thinking that you just need to try harder. Maybe you feel it in your shoulders, or with the migraine you get on Sunday nights. It would make sense that this external stuckness is something you think you need to take action on. But what I'm proposing is that you may need to grieve first.

What if it's not the external circumstances that are keeping you from moving forward, but something internal? Maybe things aren't feeling right at work because something in you has shifted. To become a new version of yourself, you may have to grieve the old version you'll be leaving behind. And when you do, things in your life will begin to change. The same principle can apply to other areas of our lives. How can we move into a new career, relationship, or role if we're still attached to the old ones? By working with grief before you try to push through, you can get to the root of the issue in a way that action alone never could.

Take a moment to breathe. Where do you feel stuck in your life? What feels like it's no longer growing or alive? What do you need to grieve?

BEYOND DEATH AND LOSS

While this principle may support you in grieving a loved one, this take is not about grief as it relates to death and dying in the conventional sense. Despite having lost loved ones and helped others work through their own bereavement process, I am not a traditional death and dying expert. In this chapter, we'll explore grieving the unmourned losses of your life that you may not be aware are holding you back. It's the stuff that keeps you from sleeping at night. The feeling that something isn't working and you can't figure out why.

These unmourned losses can be the unconscious attachments that are at the root of your lower back pain, or the underlying cause of why you keep sabotaging your relationships. We remain stuck in life because we are stuck in our past. We repeat the same cycles because we are trying to complete unresolved issues from long ago. Remember my inner girlfriend? Griefwork was one of the ways that I was able to embody my new role as a fiancée and eventually as a wife. When you consciously work with the principle of grief, you get to experience what is beyond the pain of loss—the joy of letting go. It's like taking off a shoe that's too small: When you lean into letting go, you'll feel the relief of making space for who you are beyond the pain of loss. That is where you will find out who you really are, an infinitely unfolding Soul in human form.

FEELING YOUR WAY THROUGH GRIEFWORK

This healing journey is not linear or logical. This is a journey that you must feel your way through. That's because much of your past is still very present in your day to day. When you feel stuck in life, you probably try to think through the problem and do more to solve it. But when you've exhausted all the options, the solutions that you find are rarely satisfying. Something I have seen hundreds of times is when a client thinks they should get a job right after they get laid off. It seems so logical. You have to make money to pay the bills, right? But when you get laid off three times in a row despite trying to do your best, you may start to realize that there is something more to the story.

Maybe your body is telling you this, too. You've had one knee surgery and three spinal surgeries before you're thirty, and now your other knee is starting to hurt. You're frustrated that you will have to go under the knife again. In this scenario, if you only use logic, you won't have the ears to hear what your body is trying to say. You can't imagine what is going on from the surface. What is under the surface of your logical awareness? The good news: It is not bad or even scary. It's a version of you that is hurting—and you can help.

If you slow down and reflect, you notice that your body is having its own response to what you're going through. Digestion issues, body pains, injuries, and so on can all be bids for your attention, not just body issues. That doesn't mean you don't seek medical attention. It means that you pay attention to what your body is trying to tell you. And you do this by seeking medical attention *and* by becoming attuned to your body in a deeper way. Here's a tip: If you feel like you can't make progress on something, be it a painful injury, a job, or a goal, ask yourself what needs to be grieved.

I start the grief process by attending to whatever I notice "feels off." In the case of stomach problems, for example, I make some space to quietly sit in private to become attuned. Sitting with my attention inward, I'll begin to *feel* the discomfort. This doesn't seem like the logical thing to do, because who wants to feel uncomfortable? However, if I let myself turn toward what I'd rather ignore, I find that the way I feel shifts. The discomfort in my stomach starts to loosen. And I begin to feel a bubbling of air, as if a pressure valve has released. When we come into these deeper states of attention, we are quite literally shifting our nervous system from sympathetic (stress) to parasympathetic (recovery). Stay there for a while and you get all sorts of downstream effects in the body as well as the mind.

I found myself in this exact situation shortly after my wedding. I started experiencing some general stomach upset that would come and go. Sometimes it felt like heartburn, and other times I'd have cramping. On the surface, at first, it seemed to be about a baguette that I ate, and I thought I was having a gluten intolerance reaction. But when I woke up at 3 a.m. (an auspicious time to explore the subconscious mind) because I was unable to breathe with the intensity of the acid reflux, I had to take a deeper look. Reeling from my upset stomach, I asked, "What is your message for me?" and instantly I heard an answer from within myself: "I'm sad." Having done this work with clients and myself for many years, I knew to just be present. To feel and to listen. "I'm sad. I'm scared. I need you to slow down." I felt a younger version of myself wanting to cry, so I let out a few tears. Almost immediately, my acid reflux began to recede. And this is when I realized that there was something much deeper trying to get my attention.

For days prior, I had ignored the psychosomatic side of things going on with my stomach, only dealing with how my body was affecting me. When I finally approached the mind-body-emotion connection of my stomachaches, I felt the sadness, and I then realized that it was my inner child who was grappling with family trauma that had been dredged up from the wedding. If I would have *only* taken a pill every few hours to quell the discomfort, I may have missed the deeper healing that was necessary. I wouldn't have heard the part of myself that was calling for me to let go of old family dynamics.

As I've said before, there are physical issues that medicine can help to alleviate and cure. And I do believe that physical symptoms need to be addressed as such. Looking back, I couldn't help but wonder if I had subconsciously eaten the baguette (that I sometimes can't stomach) just so I could get my own attention on something that had been bothering me for weeks. Had I rejected the voice that said, "I am sad," I would have missed the opportunity to move through the grief that was surfacing and that had to be dealt with. Now that I was aware of this bigger message, I could begin to move through the grief process by moving *toward* my sadness. And what I found was a little Millana who was ready to let go of some family ties. When you become attuned to what's true for you, it's not about being accusatory or aggressive, but about honestly and directly coming face-to-face with whatever needs to be addressed, regardless of the possible outcomes. As we saw in the principle of love, this is what real self-care looks like.

In this case, my upset stomach arose from the sadness that my inner child felt with the recognition that my parents were not able to show up the way I needed them when I was a child. From the logic of my adult perspective, I thought I was over all that. But in being present with what my inner child was sharing with me, I realized that my recent marriage celebration had brought up all kinds of old painful feelings about family and my relationship with my parents. Sometimes these deeper messages can be hard to catch. Grief can come up even in the happiest of times, and having mixed feelings about your family is one of the most universal human experiences that we rarely speak about.

Until you do this kind of healing work, it's hard to see how the ungrieved losses of early childhood can be at the root of the issues that face you today. But because you were a kid when these original wounds occurred, there were few words said and little you could do about it all. So maybe you keep unconsciously playing out the same dynamics with your female mentors or friends that you had with your mom, even if it feels horrible. Or you numb your loneliness with alcohol and social media, even though you know it's not good for you. Perhaps "daddy issues" weren't something you became aware of until your thirties.

Regardless of your history of things "not working out," I know that you're a good person, and you are doing the best you can. When you have no idea that these patterns and feelings are the ungrieved pains of childhood, you think you should work harder and try more. But what remains is the feeling that something is missing. So pause right here and ask yourself these questions: What is a pattern that hasn't been working for me? What is a recurring health issue that I can't seem to get to the bottom of? Could this be related to something that I am still holding on to from childhood that I felt I never got? What are some of my ungrieved losses?

If nothing comes to mind, your body will help to point you in the right direction if you tune in. But you have to feel it in order to free it. You start with what you feel burdened by right now. Whatever you notice first, that can be the starting point. As you tune in, the energy moves and information reveals itself. When you remain open and present, your younger parts will come forward to begin to let go of their burdens. As you continue to lean into whatever comes up in your mind, body, and emotions, your perspective on the situation will shift. Less burdened by the pain and fear of your personal history, you'll start to see the situation and yourself the way your Self does. By holding your attention there, you'll start to transmute the pain into the fuel that empowers you.

As novelist Clarice Lispector wrote in *Near to the Wild Heart* (2012), "Today's pain will be tomorrow's joy. There is nothing that escapes transfiguration." Transfiguration is made possible by grieving. And tapping into an altered state through breathwork or meditation helps you to see how you can make use of what you have been through. This level of objectivity is something that our humanness has a hard time understanding. When I work with this process for even just an hour, I change as a person. I've gone from seeing myself as the victim of childhood trauma to making new meaning that serves me. It was this process that allowed me to go from being suffocated as a child to becoming a breathwork teacher who deeply honors the power of breath. For years, I abandoned myself because the pain of my past overwhelmed me. It wasn't until I learned these principles that I was able to work with the pain as my ally. All of the seven principles helped me to get here, but grief was one of my finest teachers.

I know that, like many of my clients, numerous readers will have experienced childhood traumas that were truly horrific. I am so sorry you had to go through that. I may not be able to be with you to hold your hand as you face your past, but I want you to know that while I may not fully understand, I am with you. I'm writing to you so that you will know that you are not facing this on your own. Over the years, I have helped clients who have grieved some of the most unimaginable horrors, so I promise you, you are not alone. Although I cannot take the pain away, I can offer a way to help transmute it. I'm not saying that grieving will make it all go away, but I do believe that this is one of the ways you can come home to yourself again. It's safe there, and you deserve to feel safe inside yourself. The remembering and merging with the Self that you are will help you make new meaning out of what you have been through. Griefwork is how you can make what you have been through for your use. It pains me to know that you may have gone through things that still haunt you. And yet I believe that grieving what you lost will help you heal and live a better life, no matter your past.

The first step is being with the pain that you feel. In doing so, you will begin to let go of your attachments. It can be scary to let things go, because you can never really know what's next. And it can be disempowering when you feel so stuck. Even if things aren't working, you have become used to the way things are. I know how dreadful it can feel to face your past. It's helpful to know that you don't have to "do" anything. You don't have to leave your family. You don't even have to tell people what happened. This is about coming back to yourself instead of abandoning yourself when you feel pain or discomfort. Feeling your pain, whether its emotional, mental, spiritual, or physical, is the first step. Take a breath.

This is about giving yourself the care, love, and attention you needed when these losses first occurred, but doing so right now. I find that the people who live the most extraordinary lives are the ones who are willing to fully grieve their past. You might stop yourself from even looking at what still hurts, because you believe you can't handle what you'll see or feel. Or maybe you've avoided the hard stuff because you fear that you'll have to do things that will make your whole life fall apart. But you don't have to leave your family or quit your job. And if you let the tears out, they will stop at some point. Start with feeling your pain and take it one step at a time. The rest will unfold from there, so trust the process. This is how you shed the past so it no longer haunts you. And there is no better time to start than right now. As my teacher Dr. Clara says, "You can't have your future if your past is still present."

While we'll explore this more in the practices described at the end of the chapter, I invite you to become present to what is coming up for you right now. I also invite you to trust that whatever is coming up in your awareness is for your good. Even what feels scary or off-limits is safe to explore within yourself. When working through the grief process, it can be helpful to work with a safe person or professional who can support you through it. We tend to avoid being present with ourselves by going on social media or by never being alone, but being present here as you read these words and notice what feelings and thoughts come to mind is a great way to start. Love yourself enough to stay with whatever wants your attention. Feel your body. When you do, you meet a natural intelligence that knows exactly what to do. Your body is built to grieve and release what it no longer needs. It knows how to cry, shake, laugh, and yawn. Let your body do its job to release the energy that is no longer healthy for you to hold on to.

This process is like moving through a one-person tunnel. Though I can't go through it with you, I can meet you on the other side. I'll call for you from there. It's where the sun is. It's where the meadows are awash with light and flowers. The tunnel will get uncomfortable at times, but if you keep moving forward, by feeling and listening, I promise it will be worth it. You can go as slow as you please—just keep going. When working with grief, you may shed tears, or maybe you'll just notice the feeling of wanting to cry, but the tears won't come. Feel that too. Maybe when you feel, you feel nothing. That's a feeling too. *Feel* how you feel nothing. The more you feel through whatever comes to mind, the more work your body will do for you. You can start anywhere: an image of a past incident or a body pain, for instance. Just start. Let the mind receive information, rather than trying to figure things out. With a little bit of faith, you can grieve to the freedom on the other side. Because grieving is a natural process that your body just needs your permission to engage.

HOW GRIEVING HELPS YOU GROW

When you grieve, you grow. When you move through the tunnel of grief, you get to become more of who and what you really are. Often grief is seen from the human experience: the pain, the suffering, and the loss. We honor that because you are human, and your experiences are real. There is another perspective that is just as valuable, and yet few people talk about it. You are infinite. We all are. So, what does it mean to let go when this is also the case? It means that it is possible to make what you have been through for your use. It means that you can move through things that are painful, and that acceptance is one of the ways you do that. Acceptance doesn't mean that you like what happened to you. Acceptance means that you acknowledge the reality of it so you can make use of it: It happened. Rather than perpetuating the unresolved pain, you can heal, release it, and make new meaning of it.

A client came to me about a relationship that hadn't been working for some time. He had a sense that his relationship issues were connected to his recurrent back pain and stomachaches. We began with breathwork, to help him get out of his head and into his body. Immediately, he started to feel a sharp pain in his lower back. I invited him to breathe into the pain rather than trying to alleviate it. As he did, he got hot and began to sweat as he became flushed with anger. He continued the breathwork to deepen his connection with the anger, and then he began to feel the pangs of sadness in his stomach. He started to sob, not knowing why but allowing the emotions to flow nonetheless. Within seconds he began to have flashbacks of his mother, who had been very abusive toward him as a child. As he moved through the painful memories, his body shook, and he coughed and twitched, releasing energy that he had held in for decades. I reminded him to keep breathing and moving forward. Courage rose in him. It's almost as if he remembered how to do this. Fully present now, he allowed his body to do all the work as his closed eyes shifted rapidly from left to right. His body thrashed, he was sweating, and howls of laughter flooded out of his body.

After a few minutes of this intensity, there was a shift in the room. A felt silence in the air. We started to get the sense that the light on the other side of the tunnel was becoming visible. He stopped breathing altogether, and his closed eyes widened as if he saw something glorious on the horizon. Tears rolled down his cheeks as he calmly said, "I have been choosing my mother again and again. My partner is just like her. She even looks like my mom when she was young. I've been trying to find a resolution ever since my mother died with girlfriend after girlfriend. But they could never love me because they don't love themselves." He paused for a moment as if someone had just walked into the scene to show him something important. "My God!" He yelled out loud. I invited him to breathe to take it all in and regulate the body. As he did, he seemingly received a message. He declared, "I was taught not to love myself. But now I see that we were all confused! My mom's here. She was taught not to love herself too!" Sobbing as if something beautiful stood before him, he continued, "But I get to change that now. . . . I do love myself! I have ended the cycle! I deserve to love and be loved by others who know this too."

What my client experienced was way beyond any logic. He had no idea that the root of his pain was withholding love from himself. He needed to grieve his relationship with his mother and the truth that he was afraid to feel. He let his body be his guide, and the rest unfolded in ways the mind would never imagine. It's the body that keeps the records of your life. The pain of loss is real. There's no getting around that. If you try to avoid the reality of the pain that you feel, you'll miss its transformative power. The pain of losing a parent is one thing that we tend to acknowledge. But often we forget that not having the love or safety that you deserved was its own loss too. It's in those few seconds of being with your pain that you can experience the shift.

My client wasn't just grieving the loss of his mother who had passed. He was grieving the love that his mother didn't give him. He was grieving all the implications that type of loss had on his life. All the relationships that he created because of his unresolved relationship with his mother. It was challenging, but it transformed him. Make no mistake, this kind of griefwork can feel like dying. But when you pass through the illusion of death, you realize that this whole process is about becoming new. We may never get to the other side of some things. Some grief will never run out. But the griefwork still brings us into a new way of being every time.

DON'T ABANDON YOUR(SELF)

When you deny your reality and how you really experience it, you remain stuck. This is why bypassing is so destructive. Over time, that stuckness becomes decay, and life becomes toxic. A client of mine came to me very upset after being on an anniversary trip with her fiancé the weekend before. One night, her fiancé started drinking heavily and began to "spill his guts," telling her that he didn't really want to be with her and that he was still rebounding from his last relationship. Despite being very direct with her about how he felt, she refused to accept what he said. She told me that she was committed to "making it work," believing that he "didn't mean what he said." It became clear that the reality of her situation didn't get to be real, because she didn't *want* to believe him or herself. We have all been there. In this case, the reality was too scary for her to grapple with. Perhaps she feared that if she were to face it, she would be alone forever. I'm sure that fears about her age, her worries about the wedding plans, which they'd already paid for, and her desire for a family were all heavy on her heart.

For now, she was not ready to accept the reality of her relationship. But she was unknowingly refusing the opportunity to let go of their old relationship that wasn't working, so that something new could emerge between them. In denying the truth of what was no longer working, all they'd get to have was a relationship that was slowly dying. That slow decay would not only affect the relationship but over time would seep into every area of her life. Over the years, this kind of decay is the very thing that my older clients have cited as the root cause of their sleepless nights, their illnesses, and their unhappiness in life.

I've had clients in their fifties who have gotten divorced after twenty-five years of marriage because, as one client told me, "My husband has been making me sick for the past decade." While no one can make you sick, holding on to unhealthy relationships can. Five, ten, or fifteen years or more of being attached to a relationship you pretend in—because you think it keeps you alive—is the kind of thing that will drain your life. Research backs this up: A sixteen-year study found that individuals who remained in long-term, low-quality marriages reported significantly lower life satisfaction, self-esteem, and health than those who eventually divorced (Amato et al. 2009). To stay in the relationship, you had to abandon intimacy and trust with yourself long before you lost it with them. When you deny your reality in one area of life, your whole life becomes a hall of mirrors. Depression, obsessive behavior, anxiety, and stress tend to follow, breaking down your mental, emotional, physical, and spiritual health along the way.

By facing the reality of what is and isn't working, you can grieve and move forward. In fact, the rupture can be the very foundation for the most ideal of outcomes. Yes, you will feel the pain of the loss of what you'd hoped for. But in feeling into not having the person or the relationship that you dreamt of, you can begin to shed your illusions and the fears that are keeping you stuck in the "not having." When you face yourself and your current reality, you open the door to real acceptance of what is and is not. This helps you to see things more clearly. Now you can decipher what is in your past from what is actually workable in your present reality.

In the case of my client and her fiancé, accepting the reality that he may have in fact meant what he said opened the door for a relationship of truth, transparency, and real intimacy. Ironically, that is what they both really wanted. In accepting that there may be truth in what her fiancé shared, they could finally be in truth, to move forward together in whatever way was best for both of them. In accepting what is, you find that the choice to build a new relationship or lovingly let go becomes possible. By being open, my client could open the door to being in a relationship that met her deepest desires. Rather than being with someone simply out of fear of being alone, she could deepen her own relationship with herself, too. You can't have intimacy, honesty, and transparency with another person if you withhold it from yourself.

That soulmate connection, the dream job that feels deeply fulfilling, the feeling of finally belonging or truly being seen, all come from finding it within. You can't feel the soulmate connection if you have abandoned your own soul. You cannot experience fulfillment if you are not fully in your truth. You won't feel at home out in the world until you come home to yourself. The feeling of being truly seen arises from truly seeing yourself. The things that you want in life, or the things that you feel are missing or lost, are found within you. Grieving what we thought was withheld from us is how we remember that.

If you only take this message in through your logic, you'll miss it. Because the process of grieving (detachment) is an experiential one that you must feel through to understand. As a human being, you will attach again and again, but the Self in you is unattached. To live the life you came here for, you must be willing to be open and let go again and again. The more you let go, the more you become. Your aliveness is measured by this infinite cycle. You attach and detach, again and again.

Grief isn't all letting go—it takes faith to trust in the process of grief. You have to have faith to make new meaning of what you've been through. Grief is how you make space for everything life hands you. The irony is that faith calls you forward to attach to something new. And yet, to have more in life, you also must let go, so that you have space for it. That is why faith and grief are inextricably tied. You work with faith to attach and become, and you work with grief to detach from the very thing you became. You cannot fully grieve without faith, just as you cannot have faith if you are not willing to grieve. Because all of the seven healing principles are interconnected, each principle will lead you to the next, and faith is the next principle because it is so naturally connected to grief. Now that you have a new relationship with what presence, love, and integration means to you, you can bring it all to the following griefwork exercises.

Practicing Grief Awareness

It's important to check in with yourself to ensure that this practice is right for you at this time. While these practices are self-led, they can bring about intense emotions and painful memories and might be best explored with a trauma-informed professional. If you have experienced complex trauma, suicidal ideation, or PTSD, I highly recommend working with a professional before doing the following practice on your own. You can find certified grief professionals at the Association for Death Education and Counseling (www.adec.org). If you are currently in a crisis or feel emotionally overwhelmed, please reach out to a helpline or mental health support service for immediate assistance. Resources like Find a Helpline (https://findahelpline.com) are available to connect you to help quickly.

Body Attunement Practice: How to Let Go of Grief Held in the Body

With this body-based practice, you will use somatic movement and breath to move through resistance into your body where the grief is held. As with the other exercises described in this book, it will be important to leave your logic at the door. Much of our grief is not "logical," so it's important not to use that metric for the validity of your experience. Your feelings are valid and provide valuable information even when they're fleeting. Your breath is key in moving through this practice. Remember, there are no "bad" emotions. When your emotions feel strong or uncomfortable, lean into them and they will shift. This only takes seconds of deep presence!

To begin, create a music playlist that's approximately thirty minutes long. Include songs that inspire movement but that also feel right for the tone of what you want to focus on. This can be anything that gets your body moving. Maybe your favorite hip-hop is what gets you in the mood, or perhaps Tori Amos's ballads are what you want. There's no right or wrong here. Just follow your gut on what will make you feel deeply.

Next, create a private space where you can move, emote, and make the faces, expressions, sounds, and shapes that you want to make freely. Close the door, cover the windows, and let those in close proximity know that you will need privacy for the full amount of time the door is closed. Dress in comfortable clothes or no clothes for free and easy movement. Have water nearby, and use the restroom before you begin so you can continue the session uninterrupted. Start the playlist and commit to movement and breath for the length of it.

For this exercise, start by standing rather than sitting or lying down. Close your eyes and breathe deeply into your belly, in through the nose, out through the mouth, with long, slow inhales and exhales. Ground yourself with your breath while listening to the music and gently start moving to its rhythm. Start small, maybe by slowly putting a bend in your knees and swaying a little side to side. Or roll your wrists and slowly swing your arms.

Gently scan your body for any sensations. Slowly breathe in what you feel as if your breath is reaching toward feeling it more. Exhale slowly, out through the mouth, as if to release what you feel. Gently notice what physical sensation calls your attention, be it hip pain, neck twitching, or anything else.

As the music plays, use your breath and body to move toward feeling your bodily experience even more. For example, try inhaling as you focus on the feeling of the stiffness in your neck while raising your arms above your head and swaying them from side to side. As you exhale, hunch over and swing your arms down by your sides. You are moving and breathing to feel more, even if it's a bit uncomfortable.

You might start to notice other emotions coming up. If so, use your breath and movement to move toward feeling these emotions more as well. You might slow down or stop the movement altogether so that you can feel them more acutely. You might begin to have flashbacks or feel the energy of a loved one near you. Allow yourself to breathe into this as well. If you feel numb, feel that too. Keep your eyes closed. Let yourself dance and stomp the floor to feel the energy flowing through you. Sometimes, you have to contrive a feeling or movement to reconnect with it. Shake and make awkward movements on purpose, and then let your body go wherever it wants, however it wants. If you don't feel silly at some point, you can likely push yourself further.

Allow yourself to notice any synchronicity between what you are feeling and thinking and what you are hearing in the music, as there tends to be an interplay that spontaneously arises. If the drumming starts getting louder, maybe your anger or sadness increases too. Don't check the clock, but instead commit to keeping your eyes closed while feeling and moving until the playlist is over.

Keep breathing, one inhale through the nose and exhale through the mouth.

As you become more and more attuned to your body, time and space will slip away. Your inhibitions will start to fall away too, and your emotions and inner wisdom will surface. Feelings of grief and fear may arise. Let yourself lean into them and notice how the quality of the emotions change.

When your playlist is over, begin to slow your movements and come to a pause. Remaining standing, place one hand over your heart and the other over your belly.

Come back to your everyday breath. Slowly inhale through your nose, filling up your belly and chest, and slowly exhale through your mouth, flushing out all the residue. Do this a few more times until you're ready to open your eyes.

Take a seat and take out your journal to answer at least these three questions: How do I feel right now? What am I ready to let go of right now? Who in me needs to speak and what do they have to say?

Repeat this exercise as often as you need to in order to reconnect with the grief held in your body, mind, and emotions.

CHAPTER 7

The Principle of Faith

You came into this world as a complete kit, inherent with everything you needed to create the life ahead of you. Just as a single acorn can become an old-growth forest, within you are the infinite possibilities of creation. Quite literally, too. Science has discovered that at the time your grandmother gave birth to your mother, your mom had all the eggs in her ovaries that she would carry over her lifetime. Your mother was holding the egg that would eventually become you while she was still in your grandma's womb. The blueprint for your life was set long before you were born. Your life's potential was just waiting for the right moment and opportunity to cocreate with your father. Just as your visions, hopes, and dreams await in you for the right time and opportunity to come to life. Faith is the portal for making the intangible tangible. It's through the practice of faith that you take what is on the inside of you and birth it out into the world.

What you create over a lifetime, though, pales in comparison to what you can become in the process. The calling on your life and the desire to achieve your goals are two different things. The calling comes from a place of wholeness, there only to realize more of who and what you already are. In contrast, a desire to achieve something, to have any specific outcome at all, will always be temporary. That is why faith isn't about getting things in life, but about a deep inner calling that inspires you to *be* who and what you truly are: the infinite veiled for a lifetime in physical form. When you explore life like this, you operate within the framework of unlimited possibilities rather than within the fear-based reality of a "not-enough and incomplete" ego.

There are levels to this concept, because no matter what your background, religion, or beliefs may be, you do have faith. Faith that the sun will rise in the morning and that you will too. That you will be able to read this next line or eat your next meal. If you have a job, you have faith that you'll get a paycheck. There is no question that you have faith. The question is, what and who do you have faith in?

At its core, faith is trust. Trust in the ineffable force that makes your heart beat and causes the sun to be the perfect distance from Earth. From Latin, the root word of "faith" is *fides*, meaning trust or confidence. It shares the same root word as "fidelity," meaning to be loyal or faithful to. And to be confident in something, one must have a deep conviction in a set of beliefs that guides one's actions. For many, those core beliefs are totally unconscious and often outdated. The principle of faith invites you to get clear on what and who you put your confidence in and asks that, above all else, you be faithful to the truth within. Pause and take a breath to let that sink in.

Let's say that, because of how you were raised, you have always assumed that you would have a nine-to-five job. You went to school so you could get a high-paying job, where you could get more time off than most people, because what you really wanted to do was travel. With a "better job," you get six weeks a year to do that. But it wasn't until someone you loved died unexpectedly that you realized you'd never even thought about how you might be able to travel without a nine-to-five. And perhaps now, waking up to the preciousness of life, you start to ask yourself what truly matters in life. So you start spending some time focusing on finding your truth. While meditating one day you get a direct message that it's time to live life to the fullest. Before you know it, you start to see videos about people who quit their jobs to follow their passion. Within the same week, you run into a friend who tells you out of the blue that they think it's time to follow your passion for traveling full time. Within just a few days, you get the overwhelming sense that the whole universe is conspiring for you. So much so, that you can no longer ignore the fact that it's time to pursue your passion for travel with your full focus.

Often, it's not until some major event happens that you start to question what you believe is true about your life. When you do, things change quickly. The truth lies in your inner calling. It calls you forward to make a life that only you can live. That is why you have dreams. They are placed on the inside of you as a personalized map to explore outside of the confines of your cultural programming and familial expectations. In connecting with your inner calling, you cocreate with the unseen forces that aim to support you in living a meaningful and fulfilling life.

Have you lost contact with your calling? Think back to what you wanted to do as a kid, but lost confidence in as you got older. When people stay loyal to their deeper calling, they often discover possibilities they hadn't imagined. But that's just the beginning. The life of your wildest dreams isn't about the house you live in or the fame you can amass. Ask Jim Carrey, the world-renowned actor, who said, "I think everybody should get rich and famous and do everything they ever dreamed of so they can see that it's not the answer" (Stone 2005). Carrey knows that faithfully living your truth is really about—self-realization. Within your dreams are the inconceivable power and privileged responsibility that comes with realizing that you are totally free and infinitely powerful.

What most people don't talk about is that faith is about the process, not the outcomes. You will get results and you will transform again and again, becoming unrecognizable even to yourself. Over a lifetime of intentionally following your truth, you will have to let go of so much, too. As you know from the principle of grief, you will constantly have to make space for the new that you allow into your life. Faith initiates an endless cycle of death and rebirth. You will "die" to your Self many times, shedding old identities along the way. That is because faith is the other side of the same coin as grief. With each new dream manifested comes the ending of a former one. Faith is attaching to an identity that you will eventually have to detach from. Faith is the attachment to the new, knowing that one day you will have to let go of it. This is why faith is about the process and not about the outcome. The outcome is always passing, but you continue to become more of who you truly are.

TRUSTING THE UNSEEN

Whether it's faith in your higher power, in yourself, or in the healing process itself, faith requires that you trust in the unseen, in something yet to be experienced by you anywhere but within your inner world. Living in your dream home, overcoming a diagnosis, or becoming a parent is the outcome that inspires you to be the person who *experiences* that achievement. Once you have manifested that result, you'll realize that it was never about that person, place, or thing that you manifested, but about what was revealed in you along the way. Every challenge and breakthrough that you experience along the way is there to help you become more self-realized. Each one reveals what you have always been but could not yet hold.

In short, faith is about waking up to your truth again and again by working with the cocreative power around and within you. That cocreative power is the same intelligence that tells the flower when to bloom and the caterpillar how to make a chrysalis. Some call it God or Goddess. Others call it Self, Source, Nature, or the Universe. Perhaps for you, God is a religious figure. Or perhaps you are open to the idea of faith as it relates to trusting in a benevolent good, but not a god in particular. No matter what you name it, you'll find at some point in life that you will have a personal relationship with it—even if that's when you pray you'll make it through a near-death experience.

Perhaps you're already in contact with your inner guidance, or in constant communication with the greater intelligence speaking to you. Either way, I invite you to name this force and recognize that you already have a relationship of some sort with it. This power seeks to know and support you in a personal way, from the mundane to the transcendent. With the principle of faith, we are going to explore this relationship within and around you. As you deepen your relationship with this cocreative power, you'll gain clarity and the confidence to move forward with faith.

MY JOURNEY OF BECOMING

I have spent much of my life depending on this relationship. Over the decades, I've come to know unequivocally that it's real.

Self is my subjective experience of an infinite greater Source, and when I surrender my trust to that relationship, an incredible transformation unfolds. I'm writing this chapter fourteen years after I won *Project Runway*, Season 8. It was Thursday, September 9, 2010, and it was a day that would forever change my life. Nearly a decade and a half ago, I rose from my bed in Harlem for the first time as the winner of a show that I'd known I was going to win before I'd even auditioned. I know it's no coincidence that I felt called to write about the principle of faith the same week as the anniversary of this momentous time in my life. And believe it or not, winning *Project Runway* wasn't what made this story worth telling here. It was who I became in the process.

I could go as far back as my childhood to talk about faith, but for the purpose of this story, I'll start with the summer of 2010. It was early July, and I had just graduated from the City College of New York. Although the city was still reeling from the great recession and most of my classmates were still looking for jobs, I was as happy as a clam. I had a part-time gig working at *Vibe* magazine in Harlem, just a twelve-minute walk from my Uptown apartment. I was also a (barely) working model/actress with more time to audition now that I wasn't a student. I had just gotten back from Houston, Texas, where I'd gone for my sister's high school graduation, when I got the call that would change my life. "You have thirty minutes to get to Parsons for *Project Runway* before they close the casting," my agent exclaimed. Standing on the corner of Twenty-Third and Sixth drenched in sweat and summer rain, I quickly hung up to be on my way. As soon as I did, I heard a voice within me say, "You are the winner of *Project Runway*." I laughed out loud, thinking, "God, can't I just go to the audition first?!" And off I went.

When I got to Parsons School of Design, I was the last one to catch the elevator as the last group of models headed to the casting room. It was an elevator filled with a bunch of beautiful young women all from much bigger agencies than mine. That didn't matter to me, though, because as soon as we exited to the main floor, I got the sense that something good was unfolding. It was almost as if there was a thickness in the room. I'd had this feeling before. It was as if there was a good spirit in the room, and I knew to trust what I felt. Before long, it was my turn to strut down the imaginary catwalk to a panel of three judges. I gave them the best walk of my life. One that I had practiced for years in the halls of my Harlem apartment building. They studied me as I did my thing and told me that casting would be booking by the end of the next day.

I went home that night with a feeling in my stomach that something important had happened that day. As I lay in my bed that night I prayed, "God, if I get booked for this show tomorrow, I will believe that what you said before my casting is true, and I will do my part to keep myself in the feeling that I am already the winner of *Project Runway*." The next morning, my agent called to let me know I was cast as one of the seventeen models to be featured in *Project Runway*'s Season 8. For the months that followed, the seventeen models would be whittled down one by one as our designers were picked off by the show's competition. We would spend as much as sixteen hours on set in a small windowless greenroom for weeks at a time, all to get to the end where three models would walk in New York Fashion Week for the season finale before being chosen with our designer as the winners of one of the most watched shows on television in the world.

From day one, I knew I had already won. The outcome was set. My only job was to live it. To do that, I spent most of my time reading, meditating, and listening to uplifting music or repeating the affirmation "I am the winner of *Project Runway*." When other models were comparing notes about who was going home, I sat quietly knowing that it was never going to be me. On the days that the drama of the designers overflowed into drama between models, I pulled back to focus on other things. Why would I compare myself if I knew that I was already the winner? One by one, I started to notice how others' attitudes had a direct correlation to their experience. The model who was sobbing about a fight with her husband the night before was the same model who would go home that day. The designer who was scared about not being good enough was the designer to get cut early. It was the cool, the confident, the excited, and the passionate who seemed to do the best and had the luckiest breaks.

But none of that mattered to me because my faith was unshakable. Until, on the third- or fourth-to-last episode, my faith was tested. My beloved designer, April Johnston, had a rough challenge, and it was made clear that she was going home. This was confusing, because that typically meant that as her model, I was going home too. But in my heart, I knew that wasn't possible. Just as the cast and crew were starting to process what was happening, the producers wrapped the day, saying there would be a new way of doing things starting the next day. I could feel the fear of the unknown seep into my mind and body, so I hurried home to encircle the doubt before it took over.

When I got home, I locked myself in my room to sort things out. Exhausted, I plopped onto my bed, aware that I'd better shift my mood fast. I knew that my job was to stay in the feeling of being the winner, but I first had to face the reality that my fear had shaken my faith. The other reality was that I had to face that it was not looking good for my designer. I began to feel that in my body, and I started frantically jumping up and down to shake off the feelings of worry and doubt. I had to let go of the "how," so

I forced myself to dance as I screamed, "I am the winner of *Project Runway*," with tears pouring down my cheeks. Exasperated, I picked up a pad of paper and a marker and wrote, "I AM THE WINNER OF *PROJECT RUNWAY*! I AM THE WINNER OF *PROJECT RUNWAY*!" again and again until I felt it in every cell in my body. Finally, after forty minutes, I was back to the feeling that I was the winner. There was no doubt, and the details of how things would work no longer mattered. I had faced the situation, and I no longer feared what was. The rest, I knew, was out of my hands.

The next day, I held my head high despite the smirks from my fellow models and the looks of pity from the crew as we few remaining models and designers were called to the runway. We were given the news that in an unusual move, the remaining designers would choose new models. The catch was that the designers' names would be drawn randomly from a bag to determine the order of choosing. One by one, each model was chosen, until it was the last designer, Gretchen Jones. Two models remained for her to choose from: me and the fan favorite Eyen Chorm.

I couldn't imagine how Gretchen would choose me over the likes of Eyen. But I closed my eyes and surrendered to my faith that I was already chosen. When I opened my eyes, Gretchen had chosen me. When they asked her why, she said I was the only model who was the exact same size as the outdated Parson mannequins. All of the other models were much smaller than me, as the model standard of that era was 0–2. And I was bigger, more like a 2–4, the same size as the older, "out of fashion" mannequins. With my exact shape and size, Gretchen knew that she would never need to worry about the fit. The patterns she had fitted to the mannequin would fit me like a glove. I had always been given a hard time about my size 4 measurements, despite how ridiculous that was. Finally what others considered a flaw ended up being my advantage. What is meant for you can never miss you.

Gretchen and I went on to walk in one of the opening shows of New York Fashion Week at Lincoln Center. And later that day, with the most gratitude I had ever felt in my life, we won *Project Runway*. It was one of the best days of my life. Despite having such a major win in the material world, I realized, *Project Runway* was a deeply spiritual experience for me. It wasn't because it was cool to be on the show and make all that money, even though that was great. It was because of what happened in the journey. I'd moved to New York knowing fewer than five people. I'd had no money except for the 30 percent annual percentage yield school loan that had made it possible for me to transfer schools without family support. Still a teenager, I'd moved to one of the most dangerous blocks in Harlem after living in an all-girls' dorm at a small university in East Texas. I'd worked multiple jobs for years, just barely getting by. And yet, despite how it looked on the outside, it was always working out for me. Becoming the model winner on such a popular show just three years after moving to New York felt like payback for all that I had been through. My faith made me become the person I saw in my dreams—and learning about the power of faith was the real reward. Winning *Project Runway* was the icing on the cake.

Over the years I've noticed a pattern in how faith works. I've witnessed it so many times with my clients that I've come to realize that these truths are universal and can work for anyone, no matter their religion, beliefs, social status, or background. Instead of viewing faith as a formula to follow, however, I prefer to think of it as a collection of ingredients. You'll mix and experiment with them in your own way, discovering the right blend with every situation you face. It's important to remember—with all of the principles—that it's always about finding what works for you. I'll share the components of faith that I've found work for me. The rest is up to you, and I promise you that finding your own way with the following components will make the journey way more fun and fulfilling. Faith is about the process and not the results, so I ask you to consider that life gets to be fun and fulfilling now, not just when things manifest later.

EMBRACING YOUR UNIQUE FAITH JOURNEY

You know how profound faith can be: Now it's up to you to cultivate your personal connection. For one of my clients, it looks like daily hikes in the forest by her house. She puts her phone on airplane mode so she can put her voice notes on without interruption. When she gets a "download," she records what she hears right into her phone. After years of this, she has a treasure trove of wisdom that she saves under themes like love or health, to listen to when that specific reminder is called for. Over the years she has come to know the difference between the voice of Spirit, as she calls it, and her own ego. It can be hard to know the difference between the Self or Source and your fears, and it may be helpful to keep the following things in mind.

Whatever you choose to call this—Self, God, or Source (I'll go with "Source" here)—it is life-affirming. It is compassionate, positive, and uplifting toward all people and circumstances. Its messages are present tense focused, yet it can show you both the past and the future. While the messages are nonjudgmental, they are also matter of fact. Source is never confused, worried, or uncertain. Even in the case of a warning, when there is danger, the underlying message is not fearful, even if you feel afraid. For example, if you were in an unsafe space, Source would be very clear about that with you without judgment. Source might say something direct, like, "Leave this place now." Over the years, I have found that while this direct communication might be surprising to the ego, the heart and body respond with relief.

Sometimes the guidance you get isn't in words, but in an intuitive understanding or feeling. Other times, it's a clear vision that plays out like a movie watched in seconds from start to finish. Whatever the case, being present and open is key. You already know how texting on your phone while you're at dinner with someone else ensures that you're not going to hear most of what they said. Communicating with Source is no different. So make time to connect with your guidance and pay attention when you get a hit on something. Trust that it's coming through for a reason and start with the following five components to do your part in the cocreative process of faith. Remember that communication goes both ways. If it's been hard to believe or even scary for you to communicate with a higher power, you can bring that up when you talk to your inner voice.

As I tell clients all the time, you can just talk to the Self or Source the way you would talk to another person. You can say how scary it feels for you to do this and how you would like to have a peaceful experience to move beyond that fear. If you don't really believe in this stuff, that's okay, see if you can at least be open.

THE FIVE COMPONENTS OF FAITH

The five components of faith are here to guide you on what only you can do so that you can allow the unseen to do what only can be done without you. I developed this handy list of the five components so that you can refer to a general framework whenever you feel lost in applying the principle of faith. You can use these to build your confidence in your relationship with your inner guidance. I encourage you to have fun with them and be experimental. Challenges and achievements are always going to be there. Remember that this approach to healing, freedom, and true power is about who you become in the process.

COMMUNICATION

The first component of faith is about relationship—specifically, the one between you and the unseen. Like any good relationship, healthy communication is how you begin. While you may not fully understand the ways of a higher power, you can still speak, listen, and relate to it, just like you do when you talk to yourself. When you connect with your inner guidance it becomes your emissary, your translator, for the larger intelligence around you. This communication can look like gut feelings, visions, a bolt of knowing, or a journal entry that feels like it wrote itself. These are extensions of your senses, guiding you to feel, see, and understand what is yet to be held in physical form.

You can build your relationship with Self (internal communication) and Source (external guidance) by speaking directly to each. Say, "Hi, Source, it's Millana. I've come to check in. What do I need to see today?" Or you can write, "Hi, Self, it's me. I heard you might talk to me if I seek you out. What do I need to know today?" Then you listen and watch for the reply—sometimes it comes in real time, sometimes in the days ahead. You might ask for guidance and have a dream, or receive a vision of, say, going to a coffee shop you haven't visited in a while. Your logical mind says, "We don't have time," but your gut nudges you to go anyway.

When you follow these cues, the world might appear different—more luminous, warm, or familiar. These are subtle signals that something—or someone—is magnetizing you to engage. You may not always know why you're being guided somewhere. Sometimes you're simply meant to sit, breathe, and observe. If a place feels off or an interaction doesn't land, it doesn't mean it's wrong or bad—just not aligned for you in that moment. Like any relationship, communication with Self and Source goes two ways. If you're distracted or checked out, the message won't land. Faith needs your full attention to work.

This kind of listening is deep and requires you to act. You can't build trust if you don't show up. You can't have a meaningful conversation if you're scrolling through someone else's life. You're not chasing signs—you're building a real relationship. That's why both listening and follow-through are so key. Each time you tune in and act, you're strengthening your ability to receive more guidance.

Sometimes the guidance you receive is quiet but clear. Maybe you're in a job that no longer fits. You start noticing friction with your team, or you feel drained every time you walk into the office. You ask Self for clarity, and then, one day at lunch, you hear an inner voice say, "It's time for you to leave." Strangely, you don't panic. You feel relief. Joy floods in—not because you know what's next, but because the truth has arrived. That feeling isn't about the outcome. It's about alignment. This level of communication asks you to trust that there is a benevolent force working with you. I've seen many clients receive guidance over and over again, but ignore it because they don't trust it—they are fearful that they are unlucky. They don't believe that their inner guidance is real. Faith invites you to believe that you and your dreams are supported—because you believe that you are supported by a loving force.

Take a moment. Tune in now with a breath. What memory, idea, or image just came to mind in the last minute? That might be your message. Faith begins by slowing down enough to hear what's already arriving. Make space. Ask. And when the messages come, act. Just like in any relationship, your loyalty and commitment are key. There is no relationship more important than the one you have with your inner guidance. You can build this relationship by opening the lines of communication to the lifeline that seeks to guide you to all that is good.

CLARITY

Once you establish communication as the basis of your relationship, you'll start to get clearer on what is true for you. As you build trust with the feeling and knowledge of your inner truth, you'll be able to tune out the influence of others. The more you're guided by the truth, the clearer your vision of your life becomes. This vision is the new reality that you are faithfully operating from. Telling myself I was the winner of *Project Runway* and then acting as such before I was cast in the series is an example of how to clarify and hold your vision. It was the point of focus that clarified all my actions. No one's opinion of whether I was winning or not mattered because my vision was clear.

Faith isn't just about the bigger clear vision, but about each step along the way. Check in every day to get clear on what the vision is today, so that you are pointing your attention and actions in the right direction. Spend time writing about what you're noticing and feeling. Feel into the truth of each moment. The truth is the guidance. What feels right? Move forward. What feels off? Then, pause and reconnect to the bigger vision. As in any relationship, you can ask for clarity and watch and listen for answers. While the whole path may not always be clear, you can trust in taking the next step that feels most in truth. As Martin Luther King Jr. once said, "Faith is taking the first step even when you don't see the whole staircase." And, sometimes, the clearest next step is all you need.

COMMITMENT

With commitment, you become what you envision. Once you establish more trust with this process, commitment is the only way forward. In the job example earlier, hearing the message "It's time for you to leave" provided the information you needed to set a new vision for your life. Even with all the unknowns that came with this initial message, you are opening up to getting more support on what is right for you. Now you move forward with a commitment to what you know is true even if you don't yet know how it's going to work out. Perhaps, after a few days of working with your inner guidance, you realize that the new vision you are aligning with is a life where you are passionate and highly valued. Maybe you don't know more than that at this point. But you can begin to commit yourself to living this new vision regardless.

At first blush, commitment does not require any action from you. It's an inner choice first. Commitment comes from being rooted in the idea that you accept that this new thing is true and right for you way *before* it has manifested in the tangible world. You don't have to know all the details to live in the reality that you're leaving your job. Or how you will be in an environment where you feel passionate and highly valued. You have simply decided that this is the new reality, and you accept it and believe it for yourself for now. You can let the vision come to you, but sometimes it's your job to decide what you are ready to accept for yourself.

When I committed to winning *Project Runway*, I was in the reality that I was the winner every day, for four months before it became my physical experience. All my actions were informed by that underlying commitment to an outcome that had yet to materialize. This commitment was between me and a greater power. Nobody knew what I knew deep inside my heart. After many years of exploring faith as a practice, I've come to understand that privacy is essential, at least at first, when you are rooting into a commitment like this. By keeping your new commitment private, you protect yourself from the natural doubts that will come when others question it. Because only you can see and feel your dreams like you can.

No one can force you to be committed. Commitment is something that only you can possess, and it occurs deep inside of you. You'll have to commit yourself to your truth again and again, because your faith will be tested. This is not because there is some evil force that seeks to destroy you, but because it's a part of the growth and transformation process as the container of your visions expands. You will feel the pressure of your dreams being in opposition with your current reality. That is why your commitment must be unwavering. Your commitment is not to external outcomes, or to the manifestation of the things that you imagine to be possible. Your commitment is in your relationship with the cocreative force that is being revealed through you and as you. Faith transforms you by revealing who you have always been. What you're truly committing to is self-realization, not the events that help you wake up along the way.

CULTIVATION

Living faithfully builds your character. With cultivation, you take responsibility for your role in the cocreation of your life. No one is going to write your story for you. Faith isn't always about ease—it often asks more from you. It's staying up late to finish the screenplay, waking up before the sun to study, choosing stillness when everyone else is going out. This is especially true when it takes years to achieve a goal. Sometimes decades. Faith is about what feels right, but you have to know the difference between what's right and what your ego wants to be comfortable.

Cultivating your dreams means being consistent with what's aligned, even when it's not convenient. There will be roadblocks. You'll be challenged. That doesn't mean you're on the wrong path. Yes, difficulty can be a signal to adjust—but it's also part of the work. Get back into communication. Reconnect to the vision. Clarify the next step. Recommit. And then—work. Cultivate your dreams like you would a garden.

Sometimes that means action. Sometimes it means stillness. Watering a garden daily might drown it. Sometimes what's needed is weeding. Drying out. Waiting. You have to be in the garden to feel what's next—just like you have to paint the painting to know what color it needs. You can't stand on the sidelines and expect the dream to arrive. You have to be in the dream to live the dream.

Cultivation is about embodiment. You take action not to become someone else, but because you already are who you say you are. You act as the person who already has the outcome—over and over again. That's how the unseen becomes real. Not through force, but through alignment.

So show up. Stay attuned. Be present. This is how you bring what's inside of you out into the world. Not all at once—but through a thousand small acts of devotion. That's cultivation. That's what makes the seed of faith grow.

CLOSURE

Closure isn't about pretending the past never happened. It's about honoring what was, blessing it, and releasing it so you can move with clarity. The fear of losing who you've been is real—but staying loyal to an outdated version of yourself costs too much. The longer you wait to close the door, the harder it becomes to walk through the one that's already open.

When you practice closure as a component of faith, you step into a deeper level of self-respect. You say: I trust myself enough to move on. I trust that something greater is calling me forward. And I choose to evolve with reverence. You're not discarding the past—you're integrating what matters and releasing what doesn't. You're no longer dragging the weight of who you used to be into the life your faith is building.

This is how faith finishes the cycle. It clarifies the vision, fuels your commitment, calls you to cultivate it—and then, finally, it invites you to release what can't come with you. Closure makes space for that. It's the last step before your new reality takes root. Faith doesn't just ask you to believe. It asks you to become. And with faith in your tool kit, you'll have the wisdom to navigate life as a cocreative process.

Practicing Faith

What is something in your life that faith can transform? What dream is calling you forward?

In the following exercises, you'll work with the five components of faith—communication, clarity, commitment, cultivation, and closure—drawing on previous practices to go deeper. These steps may stir emotion and energetic shifts, so take your time. Give each part your presence and care. Ground yourself before and after every practice. The job, the partner, the house—those things will come and go. But faith is what shapes who you become.

Step 1: Communication

- Set an intention and begin with the breathwork described in Chapter 3 on presence.
- Do the "Meet Your Self" practice in Chapter 4 to establish a connection with the Self and any other parts that are showing up. But this time, ask for guidance on a dream or goal that you have in mind.

Step 2: Clarity

- Journal what you understood in your conversation with Self about your vision or goal, and bring the conversation with Self to the pages of your journal. Do the integration practices from Chapter

5, focusing on the Self and any parts if you sense resistance.

- Ask the Self to guide the journaling session and provide clarity on what is true for you on this matter. What needs to shift internally to move forward? Are there any parts of you that are in opposition? What must be let go of? Have the Self guide you on what parts need help, and work with them on the page as well.
- Take space to let the new insights settle. Record any signs, feelings, or visions that arise in the days that follow. These are the components that create the container that you will direct your attention to.

Step 3: Commitment

- Bring to mind the vision that you've been clarifying. Do another journaling session with the Self and parts that come up related to this vision. Now that the truth has been clarified, it's time to make commitments based on what's true for you. Journal about the commitments you will choose to keep in becoming the person that lives out this vision. Get specific on actions you can take and ways of being that are in congruence with this new version of yourself.
    - For example: I am committed to being the author that I have always dreamt of. I am committed to honoring this dream as my reality.

- Create a private declaration of your commitment.
  - For example: I am committed to no longer drinking alcohol so that I can have a clear mind. I am committed to writing my book proposal this year. My book is my priority, and I work on it every day. I no longer need permission or validation from an agent or a publisher to write my book. I move forward knowing that this book is mine to write and that is what I am committed to doing.
- Write affirmations in present tense.
  - For example: I am writing my first book. I enjoy writing every day.

Step 4: Cultivation

- Now that you are clear on your commitments, list three daily actions that align with being this version of yourself. Don't overwhelm yourself. Start with the foundations that help you to be the person that can perform the actions required.
  - For example: I wake up early to do my morning practice. I work on my book every weekday from 6 to 8 a.m. I take a walk around the neighborhood every day. I stay off social media until after I have written two pages.
- Schedule specific times for these actions and schedule out larger monthly, quarterly, and yearlong commitments. Put them in your calendar.
- Note how these actions make you feel in your body.

- Track synchronicities and signs in a journal. Communicate with your inner guidance as needed.

Step 5: Closure

- Do another session with the Self and parts that come up related to this vision. This could be a freewriting journaling session. This time, identify what you need to let go of and ask for suggestions by simply asking the Self and your parts.
    - For example: In journaling with Self, you might write, "What do I need to let go of in order to move forward in my commitment to write my book? What actions and rituals might help me to fully let go of what no longer serves my process?"
- Use the grief practice to release what you're moved to let go of. Adapt it to suit the aforementioned insights and provide support for whatever your parts need as you do so. Remember, these practices can bring up strong emotions and painful memories. If you feel overwhelmed, give yourself permission to pause, ground, and seek support from trusted professionals or community.
- Work with your inner guidance to create a closing ceremony that resonates with you.
    - For example: Light a candle to begin the ritual. Draw your anger on a piece of paper, write a poem, or create a piece of art that holds the

energy of your anger. Then bury the paper in the ground. Or you might burn something in a firepit, release something into water, or create something that represents release and transformation.

- Close the ceremony with grounding practices. Speak out loud that the ceremony is finished. Take a shower or bath afterward. Hydrate and prioritize nourishment and sleep.

CHAPTER 8

The Principle of Joy

After all my years of guiding breathwork with thousands of people all over the world, the number one thing I've seen people resist the most isn't their sadness or even their anger, but their joy. Without some real nudging, it's rare for people to allow themselves to feel the all-encompassing experience of rapturous joy. In group breathwork sessions, this phenomenon is even clearer. Once the group gets going, most people eventually cry, while others yell and moan. After a while, in what seems like a room full of suffering, a few people in the room start to struggle to hold back a smile. With the exception of experienced practitioners, most people quickly replace any feelings of joy with guilt when in a room filled with people crying.

Nearly every time I come over to those struggling to feel joy, they say the same thing: "How can I feel joy when everyone is suffering?" I reassure them, "This is the ultimate metaphor for why humans resist joy. When, in fact, it's by allowing yourself to feel joy that you help others to do the same. If you want to help them, open yourself to joy first." Sometimes they'll start to smile, and then laughter will uncontrollably burst out. Like ripples in a pond spreading across the room, the joy spreads. The next person in the circle, a woman who has just been crying about her mother who has passed, starts to laugh while sobbing. A man who was yelling about his father, who beat him as a child, breaks out into happy tears, realizing that he is free of oppression. Just like that, without a single word, joy makes sense of things in the room that no one had access to just seconds before.

It's in seeing this happen time and again that I have come to realize that joy is one of the most vital aspects of the healing process. Without joy, I promise you, you will not want to continue. In healing, or in life. But joy isn't about external circumstances. Joy is intrinsically who and what you are. Most people get lost because they seek happiness in life rather than joy. Happiness is fleeting. Joy is a state. Happiness is about the happenings, and joy is unconditional. Joy is always there, because it is the feeling of the Self in the body. You don't need to do anything to have it or deserve it. Joy is about opening to the good that already exists so that you can see the world from a higher point of view. Happiness is what you seek when you feel like something is missing; paradoxically, joy is the realization that nothing is missing. When it comes down to it, joy stems from your deep appreciation for life itself.

UNDERSTANDING JOY: BEYOND FLEETING HAPPINESS

At the heart of things, all of the seven principles have one goal, and that is to merge with the wholeness within you. Joy is what your body feels when it meets the ineffable appreciation that the Self has for living through you, as you. Out of that outpouring of energy comes your aliveness. It is what tethers you to your physical form. When joy is totally cut off, so is your inner aliveness, and eventually, your will to live. Think of a time that you have felt the most alive in your life. How joyful were you? What about the time in your life when you didn't want to live anymore? I'd imagine that joy felt nowhere to be found. Our vigor for life is our connection to the Self's appreciation for the opportunity to live this one and precious life as you. Whether you're conscious of it or not, the more you are connected to the Self, the more you feel that joy. When people are joyful, they are grateful and beaming. They stand upright and their bodies convey openness. When they are cut off from joy, this, too, shows in their bodies and faces. Their faces will dim and their stances appear closed. You know what that looks like intuitively, and you can feel the difference in yourself, too. The former is life-affirming, the latter, diminishing.

Sometimes it doesn't feel that easy to get in touch with joy, though, and that may be because you have been disconnected. You reexperience joy by moving toward what you truly appreciate about being alive. By honoring what lights you up, you attract more of what you value, because what you appreciate appreciates. When you feel disconnected, you have a task before you: to begin uncovering and moving toward what you truly value. Cultivating a sense of what you value in life means that you have to get back in touch with your inner guidance and get clear on what is authentic in you rather than focusing on what you "should" like or "have to" do. Over the years, I've seen that it's the "shoulds" and "have tos" of life that lead to disconnection from what truly enlivens you. It's the programs and expectations of your family, community, and culture that point to a path to achieve temporary happiness rather than intrinsic joy. Joy is uncovered in the process of living according to your true nature and deepest reason for being.

THE KEY TO FINDING WHAT'S ALWAYS BEEN AVAILABLE TO YOU

If reconnecting to your joy sounds daunting or impossible, I assure you that it's the most natural thing you could do. Think about the joy that children have. Why do you think most kids are so joyful? People often say it's because they have no responsibilities or bills to pay, but I would challenge this notion. It's because children have yet to be indoctrinated into our cultural belief that you need something in order to enjoy yourself. I was watching my friends' kids a few weeks ago, when they came to join my husband and me for a picnic in the park. At first, they were shy, and almost immediately ready to go home, but within a few minutes of exploring the park, they met other children and began playing on the grassy area by our picnic site. The next thing we knew, they were carrying old cardboard boxes around with plastic astronaut helmets on their heads. They held hands with their new friends, gathered sticks, and wrote maps in the dirt to chart the new journey in their spaceships. They'll likely never see each other again, and yet they played like lifelong friends.

This is what joy looks like, and this is what it means to be alive. It's natural and has no agenda. No needs to be fulfilled other than what is immediately in front of you. My friend's kids didn't need to sit down and think about what they were grateful for—they just took advantage of what was available and had fun with it. They went after what they valued most. This state of innocence is there because they're enjoying what is right in front of them—with no guidance, influence, or direction. Watching them, I could see that these children were still in touch with the creative and joyful Self. If given the space and safety, kids get into the natural flow of their childlike wonder and ability to play. The good news is that you are still that child—you just have a bigger body. You are that little kid who can follow the intuition and creative urges that never left you. The only difference is that now, you are also the adult who is remembering that part of yourself, so that you can be the adult you always needed, too. With this principle, you are invited to return to your childlike joy and sense of wonder as a way of life. You'll do that by letting go of old habits and beliefs so you can begin having fun again.

REDISCOVERING JOY IN ADULT LIFE

You might be thinking *Who has time for that?* or "How can I play all the time and be the one who pays for it all? I have to work!" Trust me, I understand. I've definitely been there. So let's go deeper into this concept. You are both the child who wants to enjoy life and the adult who can create the space and resources to do so. Play is what you do with your joy. Usually, when you "grow up," you become serious and leave your playful innocence behind. This tends to come from the belief that fun is something you put away so you can handle life. But this principle offers you a new point of view. If joy is always present, what might it look like if joy was prioritized? What would your life look like if your adult life was reoriented with joy in mind? How would you look at life if everything was a game that had no rules? Breathe for a moment and really consider it. This is what we are going to explore.

Disclaimer: You are going to come upon people in your life, even close friends and family, who will be really triggered by this approach to life. It's very likely that you yourself have internalized them. This is "the hater" archetype, if you will. We all have a serious internalized "adult" who is trying to keep us safe from harm. A well-meaning part is trying to keep you safe from poverty, or from being ostracized. Whatever the case, the idea of living life with the wonder and innocence of a child can seem threatening. And this doesn't just come from outside of us; it also happens within your own psyche.

I'm flagging this now because integration of those parts is key to forging ahead on the joyful path. It's also important to remember that joy is not the same as happiness. Joy is not circumstantial. Joy is a state that is always there because it's the way the Self feels within you. It's a present state, so when you start thinking that you will only be able to have joy when conditions change, you know you have gotten off track. Joy can never be because of or in spite of something or someone else. It's bigger than that. Joy has the power to hold all emotions. Fear, anger, and sadness can still be there in the midst of joy—they're just no longer the loudest voices in the space. When you start moving toward a life that is more authentic, because it's aligned with your values, the serious adults and haters within and around you will show up. That means that living joyfully is also about a willingness to be different, both from others and from former versions of yourself.

JOY OPENS YOU UP TO RECEIVING MORE

When opening up to joy, you are reconnecting with who and what you really are. Think about the one friend or family member who you have the most fun with. If you're anything like my sister Jill and me, you spend most of your time laughing so hard that you cry. When she and I are together, it's like we're kids again. Everything is fun and incredibly hilarious. Whenever we spend time together, I walk away feeling like I was more myself than I've been in a long time. It wasn't until a few years ago that I realized that I could let myself be that way anytime and not just when my sister was around. That level of joy, wonder, and playfulness not only keeps you young, but is incredibly magnetic. When you allow more joy in your life, an interesting thing happens. Your life starts to get better and better. The more you are in touch with your true Self, the more authentic you are and the better you feel about yourself. And the better you feel about yourself, the more the world starts to reflect that joy back to you. My clients and I often notice that more opportunities appear when they feel joyful.

This is where the principle of joy gets really fun. The "nothing is so serious" kind of joy that you are connecting with in yourself is the very thing that will help you receive more, and without more work. Think back to when you were most joyful and appreciative of your life. Didn't the world feel like your oyster? Did you think everything was so serious? I bet if you think about it for a second, you'll remember that more opportunities came your way when you were already enjoying life. If you really think about it, you'll remember it's a choice, not a result. When you feel burdened by the seriousness of adulting, with responsibility heavy on your mind, it's likely that you'll stop having fun. I have seen it so many times both in my own life and with my clients.

The trick is to remember that joy is experienced in the body. When you attune to what your body is telling you, you attune to where the Self is guiding you to flourish. That isn't always "logical," because the wisdom of the Self is bigger than what makes sense. Joy doesn't come through "figuring things out"; it comes from being in the moment. Joy is experienced in the here and now and builds momentum as you lean into it. Because the Self has no agenda or concept of lack, following your inner guidance makes life feel more like a river flowing downstream than a struggle upstream. Rather than just fulfilling your to-do lists, you find pleasure in daily tasks. That means getting out of your head and your list of "shoulds" and into your body and the moment.

You will need to start feeling your body's responses to know what direction to take. For example, say an old friend texts you to go out for dinner on a night that you happen to be free. You reach to text back but feel a twinge in your stomach when you think about how every time you hang out with her, you leave feeling drained. You may briefly sense the dread of spending your one free evening this week with her, but you text her back a yes because you feel bad telling her no. This is the perfect example of how you might currently be orienting your life around what you "should" do. Perhaps you think that you should sacrifice your time and energy to being a good friend. That may somehow seem logical. But how does that stack up to an internal feeling telling you to say no? The body is telling you what's right for you, but the fear of being disliked has won out. You can see how making "logical" choices all day long that feel bad internally could lead you to disconnect from your inner joy. They add up to a life that feels like a farce.

Try tapping into how your body feels instead. In my household we have a guiding affirmation for this: "It's only a 'yes' if it's a 'hell yes.' And it's 'hell no' if it's anything but 'hell yes'!" In short, if you're not fired up about it, it's a no, and this is where things get real. You may find out that the reason joy has evaded you is not because you're not doing enough but because you have said yes to things that are not a match for who you really are. This realization can be challenging, because you might start to notice that much of your life will have to shift if you're going to stop doing the things you feel obligated to do. Perhaps you will have to quit a job that you hate because you feel sick every Sunday night thinking about going back into the office. Perhaps it is time to take that painting class that you have so badly wanted to enroll in, despite the fact that none of your friends want to join you. There will be people you will need to say no to and opportunities you will have to summon your courage to show up for. The good news is that you can start with the small things so that joy's life-affirming energy can give you a boost of confidence as you keep going forward.

To be clear, I'm not telling you to quit your job or abandon your family. That is often what my clients jump to when we have this conversation. Let's dig into the nuances here. Joy is about moving toward things in yourself before moving away from things in the external world. Joy *includes* our more challenging feelings, so bypassing difficult emotions isn't the path either. Feeling the emotions while focusing on what is calling is how this works. Gratitude is the skeleton key. You start by focusing on what you love and what feels aligned, rather than pushing away or ending what isn't working. But you don't deny what isn't working. You include it. You grieve it. You become present with it. And in that process you open up to your practice of faith, in order to open up to what is calling you. Without having to leave or quit anything, you change your relationship with it. Then your actions will begin to reflect that change.

You might be saying, "But you just told me to stop doing what feels bad and move toward what feels good! And that would mean leaving this job / these people / this situation that I hate." Yes, joy calls you toward what lights you up—in the moment. Sometimes in the moment that means leaving an unhealthy situation because it's gone too far. But joy is not conditional. To have real joy, you must focus inward first. It's a sham to think that your external circumstances are keeping you from being joyful, and that changing them will bring you joy. That is conditional living, and joy will always evade you that way. When you change the way you feel about your circumstances, your circumstances can change. Take action once you have become resolved within yourself and your actions will lead to a much higher path. Otherwise, I assure you that a similar issue will follow you to your next job or relationship.

"Bloom where you are planted" by making new, more positive meaning about why you're in this situation. Affirm it. Accept it. So that you can build the energy and insight to make the right actions out of joy and gratitude rather than spite and bitterness. It's the difference between being called and inspired forward versus fighting and struggling in something that you believe is holding you back. Making this shift will wildly impact the actions you take.

I knew a guy years ago who hated his job. He worked at an electric company in New York and was just a couple of years away from getting a larger pension. So instead of quitting, he decided to enjoy working there while he bided his time. Instead of working himself to the bone, he took up all his vacation and sick days and went places he always wanted to visit. One day, he confidently told his boss that he was going to start working new hours, and his boss, surprisingly, agreed those hours would be better. Before my friend knew it, he was coming and going as he pleased and started to enjoy his time at work. Within three months he was offered a generous raise and promotion. For the two years that followed, things at work just got better and better. With the extra time and cash, he bought some local property just as the market was starting to surge. By the time he got his new benefits package, he and his mother had two brownstones in Bed-Stuy just as the Brooklyn real-estate market popped. He left his job on great terms with a better pension than he could have ever imagined, and he now lives as a semiretired local real estate hero.

Of course, not everyone can take so much time off from work or set their own hours. Sometimes, instead, you find joy in the midst of the task itself. Joy can be found in any job if you bring your full presence and attention to it. Sometimes it means refocusing on what drew you to this job in the first place. Joy comes as a complete kit. It has everything within it for everyone to benefit from. You just have to keep opening to the joy within to find out how good life can get from right where you are.

THE POWER OF APPRECIATION IN CULTIVATING JOY

Allowing joy is a practice. To practice something, you have to be willing to put in the reps before seeing results. When it comes to joy, the invitation is always about the intrinsic rewards rather than external ones. When I was writing this book, each principle presented itself in my personal life so that I could know it more deeply firsthand. The principle of joy came to me in a way that I hadn't planned. I was in the early stages of the creative process and was having a wonderful time. But in the fifth month, when it came time for me to actually put the chapters together, I realized I was in way over my head! I didn't know it at the time, but I had entered a stage in the creative process known as the "trough of despair," and it's as painful as it sounds. After the initial high of inspiration for the book, I started to realize that my writing skills were nowhere as refined as I hoped. Upon realizing how much I still had to learn to deliver a book worthy of my readers, I was struck by a wave of doubt and a deep sense of insufficiency.

Even though I was writing every day, I was struggling to get any of the pages to make sense. After a few dreadful weeks of this, I hit a new low, which felt particularly painful. At this point, I was a mess. I was doing what I thought I "should," but I was not having a good time, and the quality of my work suffered. By the sixth month, I had fallen into what can be best described as the dark night of the soul. I was no longer only questioning my ability to write a good book, I was questioning my very self-worth. I cried almost every day, wondering how I had misjudged my abilities so badly. I knew I had to finish the book, but I spent every day questioning myself instead. At night, I sobbed about how I was no match for such a blessing, because I imagined I was going to spoil whatever it was that I was meant to do.

Then one day, out of the blue, an invitation came from a high-profile media group to lead a large breathwork session on, of all things, *joy*. I would have laughed out loud if I'd had it in me. My husband and I were on the coast of Northern California at the time, so I went for a solo walk on a lonely stretch of the beach to process it all. Sobbing in the foggy mist with my hair blowing in every direction, I berated myself. "I can't even write a book on the one thing I care most about and now I'm being asked to teach about joy while I feel like this?!" Like a lightning bolt, it hit me: I was missing joy from my life. I realized then and there that the whole writing process had become about responsibility and being good enough, instead of being in awe of the opportunity to learn and grow in such a wonderful way. I had burdened myself with an ideal of perfection and the need to prove that I was worthy of the opportunity before me, rather than being grateful and enjoying the process as I learned.

What's more, I realized that I wasn't just missing joy in my own life and creative process, but I was missing joy as one of the principles of healing and transformation in the book. Now, still walking on the beach thinking about it all, I laughed out loud with windswept tears still on my face. I have always said to my clients that joy is an essential ingredient in the healing process. That joy transforms you. Because the creative process and our healing journey are pretty much identical, it was no wonder that the same thing that I forgot to include in the principles was the one thing that I needed the most. This realization opened the door to feeling a rush of joy right there in the moment. It was almost as if all this struggle that I had experienced for the past month and a half was so I could get to the realization of what joy really is. In that moment on the beach, I understood that joy had been there in me the whole time—I just hadn't let myself feel it. I'd been weighed down with the seriousness of wanting to achieve something or be something, rather than receiving the blessing that was already available.

FINDING JOY IN DIFFICULT CIRCUMSTANCES

So how does joy and gratitude work when you're dealing with tough times, illness, or poverty? Joy, like all the principles of healing, is about transforming yourself to change your circumstances. Sometimes, the diagnosis remains the same. Many people around the world continue to live in poverty even while expressing joy and gratitude for what they have. One might wonder—What is the healing power of joy, of anything, when pain still persists? But that's the mystery and grace of it. Suffering is a given in life, and yet joy can hold that, too. Even in pain that won't go away, even in the problems that persist, joy elevates the mind and body.

Studies show that gratitude practices improve mental health, sleep, and emotional resilience even when life circumstances don't change (Kase et al. 2021). Terminally ill patients often report that their illness brought them a deeper connection to life than they had ever known before—sometimes even saying they're grateful for the disease because it awakened something in them they hadn't realized they'd been missing (Teng et al. 2022). It's as if the illness itself gave them the life they didn't know they had and sparked the will to fight for something they hadn't been fully living. This might be why research shows that joy and other positive emotions create an "upward spiral" that builds psychological resources, such as resilience and meaning, even during suffering (Fredrickson 2001). Often, it's the presence of suffering that pushes us to focus on what matters most. That's the freedom joy can offer—it doesn't erase pain, but it transforms the one experiencing it.

If you are going through it in your health or with an ordeal of any type, jumping straight to joy would be a false start. Real joy is unearthed, not fabricated. In the wake of immense loss or suffering, it can seem that joy is far from reach. But it is in the little things that open at your feet, otherwise unnoticed, that are calling for your attention, where you can find joy. Nature is the best teacher for such a revelation. Nature will remind you of the everlasting power of life that flows through you and all things. Sitting on the bare open ground and listening to the hum of the Earth's power will gently help you become attuned. I believe this is why so many of us believe in the messages of our loved ones in the form of plants or animals. Spend enough time outside the city limits, or even under the canopy of an urban forest, and you will recall the joy that enlivens all things. In attuning yourself to nature in the smallest of ways, you might remember that there is a whole living world that you are very much connected to but forgot about.

Childlike play and laughter can be just what the doctor ordered. Joy is what helps you hold all of what you're going through with grace, not in spite of it, but with it. Whether you're moving through one of the most painful times of your life or simply feeling disconnected from joy, you can uncover it within yourself. Open yourself up to the good. No matter what is happening around you, there is often something good to notice, however small. Not to bypass the hard parts, but to spark something new alongside it. Start with gratitude and appreciation, and make it a regular practice. Gratitude tends to attract more to be grateful for.

Don't stop there. Be like a child and find ways to play and be spontaneous. Make space for being silly. Keep tuning in to your body to notice what lights you up so you can say yes to it. If you've made a commitment to something that feels draining, you might tell yourself that the only way you'll do it is by finding a way to make it fun and then keeping that promise to yourself. Keep focusing on what feels right and what you're grateful for, and over time, you may notice your life beginning to flow with more ease.

Next, you will find some simple but potent practices for joy. Take your time and practice at least one of them a day as you play with this principle. Within a week you'll begin to notice a difference in your overall mood and things will start to flow. I'm going to remind you, again, that you will have doubts about being responsible when you are called to have fun. Notice these doubts and fears and write them down so that you can use the other principles to work with those parts of yourself. Joy will help you to remember how important knowing your personal truth is. Be sure to slow down so you can listen to the Self and your body. You will have times where logic and guilt will try to take over. Know that all feelings are allowed at the table. Inside of you there is a child who just wants to have fun. Now is your chance to become the adult who gives yourself the life that you've always dreamed of.

Practicing Joy

Meet Your Joy

Revisit your breathwork practice at the end of Chapter 3, this time to reconnect with your inner joy. Perhaps you create a playlist to guide you through songs that bring you joy. Remember to set an intention and perform a grounding practice to begin and close the practice.

Refinement of Values

You cultivate joy when your life is in congruence with your values. Follow up the breathwork with a journaling practice on what the following themes mean for you personally, professionally, in your relationships, and in your environment.

Set a timer for thirty minutes to start, so you can't ruminate too much. Do a lightning round session of sorts, writing just a sentence or two for each question per theme.

For example: Adventure means I'm really living my best life. Adventure looks like I am trying something new once a month in my relationship. Adventure brings me joy when I see something that I didn't know existed.

What does ________________ mean to me?
What does ________________ look like in my life/relationships/work/environment?
How does ________________ bring me joy?

Adventure
Art
Balance
Collaboration
Community
Compassion
Creativity
Curiosity
Danger
Empowerment
Fame
Family
Forgiveness
Freedom
God
Gratitude
Growth
Health
Intimacy
Joy
Justice
Legacy
Love
Money
Nature
Peace
Power
Purpose
Resilience
Respect
Responsibility
Sex
Trust
Truth
Understanding
Wisdom

Journal further about the themes you noticed. What do you find you value the most in your life at this time? To integrate these values into your life, bring one to three of the themes that stand out that give you the most joy and adapt them to the faith practices to explore the core values that you realized bring you the most joy.

CHAPTER 9

The Principle of Rest

DESPITE SPENDING ONE-THIRD OF OUR LIVES SLEEPING, MOST of us have no idea how to truly rest. Like breathing, rest is essential—but most of us were never taught how to do it properly. We confuse rest with sleep, zoning out, or doing nothing. But real rest is more than physical. It's about being at rest *within* yourself—mentally, emotionally, spiritually, and physically.

Rest reconnects you to the Self—the source of your aliveness, creativity, and restoration. It's what helps you generate energy, not just replace what's been drained. Think of your body as a laptop. Most people are running on 20 percent battery at best, barely recharging overnight. Then we spend the day giving away what little energy we have: 5 percent to perform at work, 10 percent to please others, another chunk to being the best parent we can be. We end up in a deficit and only plug in when we're about to crash.

Real rest is different. It's like staying connected to the charger—not just when you're depleted, but as a way of life. When you're truly plugged into your Self, your energy overflows. You move from surviving to thriving, creating, and expanding. You have life force brimming out of you, ready to be shared. You become radiant, clear, and grounded. You feel lighthearted, inspired, and full of vitality. And then something funny happens: New opportunities to share that energy flow to you, and you have the capacity to meet them, because you are resourced from within.

When you're disconnected from yourself, you rely on unsustainable sources—sugar, scrolling, coffee, vacations—to refuel you. But these quick fixes can't replace a true sense of internal connection that enlivens you. In a culture of constant noise, we fill every quiet moment with content, messages, or tasks. We give away our energy to things that rarely give it back. Then we wonder why we feel exhausted, overstimulated, or numb. And this level of disconnection shows up in all kinds of ways that we don't realize. Maybe you've worked yourself into "success" but sacrificed your peace. Maybe you've lost yourself in a relationship or in the hustle to prove you're a good person. Maybe you party to feel alive, or people-please to feel anything at all. No matter how it plays out, the result is the same: burnout, depletion, and a loss of connection to the life force that makes you feel truly alive.

But when you work with rest as a core value in your life, you begin to restore yourself from the inside out. Yes, better sleep matters. Sometimes exhaustion really is just sleep deprivation. But I've found that my deepest rest comes not from eight hours of sleep, but from returning my attention inward to untangle myself from a draining situation. When I feel scattered, anxious, or out of integrity—I check in to see where I've abandoned myself. Because that is often where the energy leak is.

As soon as I tend to that in myself, rest comes. It comes from reconnecting to what makes me feel whole within myself. When you focus on rest from a holistic body, mind, and spirit approach, your nervous system calms. Your mind quiets. Your emotions begin to settle. Rest is not just recovery—it's a return, a spiritual digestion of everything you've taken in but didn't have the space or time to process. When you let rest do its job, it will restore you back to your inner power and reconnect you with the life you're here to live. In this chapter, we'll explore the two different types of rest and how to reclaim it as a powerful, generative force.

This power is so important because life will eventually lead you to rest. If you don't choose it willingly, it may one day choose you. I've seen clients hit walls, lose jobs, fall ill, or face breakdowns—only to realize, in hindsight, that life had been trying to slow them down all along. When rest becomes a regular part of your life, you don't need to be shaken into stillness. You meet yourself there, every day, with purpose.

THE TWO TYPES OF REST

There are two types of rest: active and passive.

Passive rest is likely the kind you know best—it's sleeping, eating nourishing food, being in nature, getting massages, or taking a calming vacation. It's the kind of rest where your only job is to stop doing. To let go. To surrender. Active rest, by contrast, is how you gain energy through intentional action. It's reading a soul-nourishing book, immersing yourself in a healing yoga class, dropping into breathwork, or getting lost in your creative zone.

It's when you're so tuned in to something that you lose track of time—you don't walk away tired, but charged up instead.

When you embrace both passive and active rest, something shifts. You stop living in constant depletion and begin to feel safe inside yourself, as though you're finally home. You draw energy from within rather than searching for it in the noisy world outside. Think back to the moments when you felt truly alive. Perhaps it was when the quiet after a long, cathartic cry left you with a sudden clarity, or when a solo walk at sunrise filled you with inexplicable warmth and purpose. Or maybe when you went sky diving and were completely in the moment. Maybe it was during a moment of wild, unguarded laughter with a trusted friend, or when you immersed yourself in a creative flow, writing or painting until the hours slipped by unnoticed. These moments weren't about escaping the world—they were about returning to yourself. They were alive because you were fully present, without trying to perform, produce, or prove anything. You were simply being with yourself, and that is what made those moments regenerative.

Passive rest heals the body by allowing it to repair and recover, while active rest reclaims the spirit by engaging your inner energy in a mindful, creative way. Together, they create a balanced state where your nervous system relaxes, your emotions settle, and your life force begins to flow freely—first for your creative use and then out into the world. And when practiced together, they restore your connection to the Self—so that rest becomes more than recovery. It becomes the foundation of a life that feels true and full of purpose.

THE POWER OF RESTORATION

Rest isn't just about sleep—it's about setting the conditions for restoration. In modern life, that takes intention. Most of us live far from natural rhythms. City noise, blue light, and stress keep our systems overstimulated. We rarely spend time in the kinds of environments—quiet forests, dim evenings, warm conversation—that help us unwind. That means we have to consciously build rest back in. Research confirms how essential this is. Studies have found that poor sleep hygiene is strongly associated with depression, daytime sleepiness, and overall impaired well-being. And they've shown that waking up early and maintaining consistent rest practices significantly improve cognitive function, mood regulation, and emotional resilience. Simply put, consistent and intentional rest practices are not just helpful—they've proven to be foundational for mental and emotional health.

For my husband and I, preparing for sleep is one of our most sacred daily rituals. We eat dinner early, keep the lights warm and low, and take a long walk at sunset to reset our circadian rhythms. We avoid screens, keep the conversation light, and wind down slowly. By 8:30 p.m., we're in bed—blackout curtains drawn, earplugs in, eye masks on, the house cool and quiet. We're asleep by 9 and we love it. It took time to build this rhythm, and it's a privilege. I didn't always have the ability to do that. Over the years, we've changed our entire lives to prioritize rest because of what it makes possible. I've written most of this book by waking up at 4:30 a.m.—clear, rested, and ready to channel what wants to come through. That window of stillness, before the world starts asking anything of me, is pure magic. It's when I feel most connected both to myself and to something greater.

You don't have to follow this exact routine, but the principle is the same: Build a rhythm that supports your nervous system. Whether you're a parent, a night-shift worker, or someone with an unpredictable schedule, your body craves consistency. Find what works for you—and protect it. Deep sleep is one of the most foundational forms of rest we have. It helps regulate mood, strengthen immunity, integrate emotions, and repair the body on every level. Your body demands it, but so does the life you deserve.

Once your body knows how to sleep well again, your dreams begin to speak. Creative downloads come. Insights bubble up. You wake with clarity, new ideas, or a song in your head. The veil between your conscious and subconscious thins, and you get to access the kind of intelligence that isn't available in your waking hours. If this all feels far off for you, start small. And start tonight. Pick just a few of the following simple sleep hygiene rituals and notice how your body responds. Then keep building from there. You'll be amazed at how much changes when your rest becomes nonnegotiable.

I have found that the following sleep routines work best for me. Take a look and see if any of them resonate with you. I'd suggest picking three of them at first and applying one each week. Make sure you journal about what you notice changes in your body and mind:

- Go to bed and wake up at the same time every day to set your body clock.
- Keep your sleeping area pitch black with no visible light.
- If you can, build your sleep gear kit: blackout curtains, earplugs, closed and locked windows and doors, eye masks, weighted blankets, loose or no sleeping clothes.
- Do your best to keep your sleeping area cool; I find that between 62 and 66 degrees Fahrenheit works best for me.
- Play brown or white noise if street noise is loud where you live. This could be a fan or even a playlist. Earplugs may work for you.

- Have water with electrolytes by your bed, but drink very little water for two hours before bedtime.
- Use the restroom right before bed.
- Try to eat dinner a minimum of two hours before bedtime.
- If you have a safe path to walk at night, take a long walk post dinner, avoiding bright lights at sundown and/or after dinner. Gentle squats and stretching can help you digest dinner, but most people find it's best to avoid vigorous workouts close to bedtime.
- Do not consume artificial sweeteners or caffeine for at least four hours before bedtime.
- Do not scroll on your phone or look at screens for at least an hour before bed.
- Keep all the lighting in your home warm and dim, preferably below your eye line, as soon as the sun starts going down at night.

Other Types of Passive Rest That Are Non-Sleep Deep Rest

- Fully allowing yourself to relax into a massage
- Engaging in Yoga Nidra, a form of meditation that uses visualization as you lie on your back (see Tracee Stanley's meditations using this technique)
- Doing a relaxing facial self-massage
- Taking a steam shower or getting into the sauna or hot tub (if not too vigorous)
- Being present in nature
- Meditating

- Doing a visualization practice
- Listening to a full calming album for enjoyment while doing nothing else

ACTIVE REST

Often clients come to me unable to sleep no matter what sleep hygiene or medical intervention they seek. This is a telltale sign that the restlessness they are dealing with is not merely physical, but related to the restlessness of their inner world. Often it's your inner parts that are at war with each other, causing mental, emotional, and physical disturbances that you only notice at night when you are the least occupied with daily tasks. More often than not, at the root of things, you are disconnected from your truth in some way, and these inner battles are subconsciously raging to be heard and resolved. Much of what is keeping you up at night is beyond your logical thinking, so these conflicts often manifest as restlessness, bad dreams, and body pains in an attempt to be expressed in any way possible. Often because of the ferocity of fear-based beliefs, you'll need to go into an altered state to allow them to come to the forefront. This is what active rest is for.

For example, a client came to me upset that he couldn't sleep, and when I asked how everything was going in his life, he said, "Everything is fine." When we got into his subconscious mind through breathwork, however, we found his inner artist was refusing to be denied any longer. My client is a passionate musician who's been privately producing music for years. As of late, he had stopped doing his music to double down on his nine-to-five career. It turned out this was because he was terrified of the implications of how good his music had become. While he was tapped into his unconscious, he heard his inner artist expressing anger: "You've been putting this off for years," his inner artist said. "If you would have just given in years ago, we would have been famous by now. Let me out! I'm ready to be heard!" My client started feeling an acute pain in his body and realized that his inner artist's anger had been building up for a long time. He then felt a wave of shame as another part of him gave way to fear: "What if I release this music and people like it?" it said. "Then I would have to quit my job. Then, I'll be just like my dad." Finally, he recognized the unrest that was what was keeping him up at night; he realized the solution was to let music help him heal the fears of his father.

The solution to the restlessness arises from a clear mind, not a stressed one. As tempting as it is, scrolling through social media before bed isn't going to help. While it can be nice to go on vacation, it's often a short-term fix, particularly if you come right back to a life that exhausts you. Leaving your family or your spouse won't "fix it" either, because wherever you go, there you are. The unrest is within you. Active rest is about making the space and time for you to sync up with the inner resources that put you in your natural state of peace—and the healing clarity it brings. Whether it's through writing a short story, making a song, or journaling with your inner parts, this kind of active rest helps you feel like yourself by reconnecting within again.

Active rest is another way for you to drop into your body and into the moment by surrendering your full attention to the present activity. A great example of active rest is the breathwork practice I shared with you in Chapter 3 on the principle of presence. Its only goal is to be more and more present by focusing on the pattern of breath while you notice what arises within and around you. In surrendering your agenda and being present with what is, you free yourself up from your ego's exhausting assumptions and habits, slowly becoming more attuned so you can hear the whispers of your inner world. If you surrender to what you find, rather than resisting it, you'll start to feel that you're in a flow, being guided by what's right for you on a moment-to-moment basis. When we drop into this state, restoration is a natural outcome.

These flow states, as they're known, can bring about a trance-like type of relaxation for your mind and body, whether your eyes are open or closed, and allow you to experience the interconnection of things. Psychologist Mihaly Csikszentmihalyi (1990), who spent decades studying this phenomenon, found that flow states happen when our skills perfectly meet a challenge. In these moments, people report feeling deeply present, clear, and connected to something larger than themselves. His research showed that accessing flow not only boosts happiness, but also supports mental resilience and emotional balance.

When in this state for even a few seconds, you quiet the analytical mind that seeks to control or fix things, and soon your ability to deal with stress increases. This state allows you to observe rather than jumping ahead or looking back out of fear—all while your immune system strengthens and blood flow increases. With this physiological shift, your window of tolerance continues to expand as your cortisol (stress hormone) levels decrease. When this combination of increased dopamine and serotonin are met with decreased cortisol, you experience noticeable benefits of restoration that continue to unfold.

Inspiration and insight arise, while fear falls away. Patterns of resistance toward pleasure melt away as well. It's as if the stressful narratives that typically hold you captive have less sway. The common fear of "Am I doing this right?" is replaced by "I am okay" instead. Your parts can begin to speak freely as you gain the capacity to handle the emotions expressed, helping you integrate memories and emotions and giving you the mental and emotional space to become more objective and self-reflective. Time and space collapse into one here and now. Synchronicity and luck abound, and former "mistakes" become happy coincidences. These are just a few reasons why rest, both active and passive, is so important for your healing work.

Now that your natural systems of rest and renewal have been fully activated, you'll begin to gain access to the higher mind while conscious. The realm in your consciousness where you have the faculties to engage the Self fully will expand. If, for example, the active rest activity is writing, you're able to write pages on end without thinking or self-editing. If making art with your hands is your active rest activity, you become one with the material, creating freely without the results in mind. In a sport such as running, you drop into a renewal state where you stop checking your time or distance. Imagine what just a few minutes a day of this could do for you. How much would your mental and physical health improve? By now, it should be clear that active rest is a kind of rest that we all need in order to thrive. When you start to make space in your life to practice active rest as well as passive rest, you'll realize that it's the only way you want to live and work.

Practicing Active Rest

Flow states happen when you immerse yourself fully in one activity at a time. Time and space blur and dilate when you fully let go and allow yourself to be taken by the flow of the present. But you have to cross the threshold beyond your ego's control before that can happen. If you can commit yourself to focusing for a predetermined amount of time or goal—one hour, three pages, five miles, etc.—your ego will have to eventually let go, because it knows how long it will be offline, so to speak. Because it can be difficult to let the ego go at first, start with the things that you know you enjoy and practice throwing yourself into the activity. If you don't know what you enjoy, think back to what you enjoyed as a kid. Or try one of the following active rest practices with your full attention every day for a week.

Examples of Active Rest to Try

- Doing breathwork with a set time and playlist in a private setting
- Taking a yoga class online or in person
- Reading to a preset number of pages or time for enjoyment
- Running or walking a certain amount of time or distance
- Making art without an agenda, with a timer set for an hour or more
- Acting out a monologue, poem, or scene
- Dancing without performing for an allotted time

- Taking action on creative impulses, intuitions, or visions as far as you can
- Freewriting for a set amount of time or pages
- Gardening with your hands
- Making something with your hands (pottery, drawings, woodcarving, knitting)
- Doing a moving meditation class such as Tai Chi
- Freely exploring a new environment while attuning to your senses
- Eating food mindfully
- Spending time in deep presence with someone who is reciprocating with deep presence, whether it is in love making, meaningful conversation, or silence
- Doing a ritual or ceremony to reconnect with the Self, the muses, and nature

Rest is one of your greatest allies. It's a direct path to coming home to your Self, to who and what you really are. Whether you're surrendering to the benefits of passive rest or taking action to begin the flow of active rest, you now know how to get to your inner well of vitality, peace, and power. While modern life will try to distract you, I invite you to take back your power by reclaiming your right to real and regular rest. Start small, improving your sleep hygiene today so you can experience firsthand the value of getting proper deep sleep. Begin practicing active rest in your waking hours by time boxing to let your ego off the hook about when it will end. As your practices and capacity to rest increase, you'll get hooked on the one thing that will give you more than it takes. The invitation here is simple: Get real rest and get it often. And your whole life will thrive because of it.

CHAPTER 10

The Journey Continues

Making Healing a Way of Life

Ever since I was a little girl, I've promised myself that I would make all the pain and heartache I went through worth it. Maybe it was through my spiritual practice or the books that I read, but inherently I knew that I would have to use what life gave me and make something good of it. I knew, even then, that it started with what I had on the inside. First it was anger that fueled my pride. Then, "I'll show them!" fueled my actions. And "Never again!" gave me the power I yearned for. When that was exhausted, my pain softened into compassion. Compassion expanded into wisdom about what happens when we heal and when we don't.

I remember being about twelve years old, in Boulder, Colorado, sitting on my bed with my best friend at the time. We had *Life* and *Time* magazines strewn about. We scratched our heads wondering how we could help in the midst of all the devastation in the world. What could we do with our lives to make a difference? What was the root of these problems in the world? After much debate, we finally came to an answer: education. Somehow, our young minds had determined that education was the basis of the change we hoped to see. But not the kind that most people get in schools. We had cobbled together a different kind of education from the novels we'd read, the ways of nature, magick (with a "k"), and a love for music, art, and beauty. We were young, but we were wise, and we still had our original innocence and love.

I see now that adult Millana is following up with middle school Millana's vision. The only difference is that I don't see this book as an attempt to educate. My hope is to help you remember what you already know, because I believe we have a lot in common. You were once a little kid with a full heart and eyes open wide. Earthside with a unique mission. I know for a fact that the radiant Self, the divine spark, is still within you. Ageless and unchanging. The Self in me is the Self that is in you too.

The inner love that is at your core is not something to be earned, but simply to be remembered. It's not some distant, unattainable ideal, but the truth that has always been within you. And it's the truth, they say, that will set you free. Because this journey back home to your Self is not a onetime thing but a way of living, a lifestyle of becoming more and more alive even as your body ages.

Breath by breath. Life will always have its challenges, but now you have a copilot: the Self. Your deepest knowing that is rooted in the Self will guide you with grace through whatever lies ahead. So build your trust in your inner truth. Spend time there. Spend time turning inward, getting to know the parts that get caught in illusion of not enough, so all of you can remember you are whole.

Take these principles and practices and make them your own. As you pull on the thread of one, you are led to the others. Grief enables transformation through letting go. Integration helps you understand that separation is an illusion as you merge with wholeness. Love nurtures growth through acceptance of your boundless nature. Rest restores you as you expand into more and more life. Faith calls you forward, by trusting the goodness of it all. Presence makes you a witness of your own thriving, leading you to the joy of the process of being alive. Through all the cycles, even resistance guides you back to Self, transcending time and space. Everything is called back into coherence.

Remember, you are not alone. As you step into your wholeness, you light up the path for others. By choosing to heal, you become a beacon, a reminder of what is possible for all of us. As you heal, we heal. And yet no one can do this task but you. When you heal, seven generations back and seven generations forward, ancestors and kin of all kinds are impacted too. You summon nature. All the living world conspires to support you in your pursuit of wholeness. Remember:

- There is nothing wrong with you that needs fixing.
- Everything you experience can be used for your growth.
- What you resist persists.
- Your body is always communicating with you.

- The Self within you is your ultimate guide.
- When something affects you deeply, pause, take a breath, and feel into its message.
- Trust your inner knowing, yet remain open and curious.

It's all within you!

Acknowledgments

I want to thank every single person I've crossed paths with in this life. However long or brief our time together, I know it helped shape this book and the learnings I share in it.

To my husband, Justin, my soulmate and life partner, thank you for being exactly who you are in my life and in the world.

To my sweet sister, Jill, you are my best friend. Thank you for always having my back.

To my aunt Mary Ann and my uncle Curt, I wouldn't have gotten far without your love and generosity. Thank you from the bottom of my heart.

To my teacher, Dr. Clara Mosely, thank you for the healing and guidance you have offered me over the years.

To my family and friends, thank you for your support and love.

To Diana Ventimiglia and the whole Balance Books team, thank you for seeing me and supporting me and this book with such fervor.

To my team, and to Craig Newman, thank you for holding this vision and helping bring it to life.

Loralei Bayette, thank you for your deep listening in the early stages. Noor Tagouri, thank you for pushing me to go deeper and reach further. MeiMei Fox, thank you for your help in the final stretch!

To all the teachers, healers, therapists, and guides I've worked with and learned from over the years, I am so grateful for the healing you helped me discover within.

To everyone who has trusted me with their healing, you are the reason I do this. Thank you.

And lastly, thank you to the Self, to Source, to Mother Earth, to my guides and ancestors, and to my younger selves, who never gave up on me, love, or healing.

References

Abbass, A., S. Kisely, and K. Kroenke. 2009. "Short-Term Psychodynamic Psychotherapies for Somatic Disorders: Systematic Review and Meta-Analysis of Clinical Trials." *Psychotherapy and Psychosomatics* 78 (5): 265–274.

Amato, Paul R., Alan Booth, David R. Johnson, and Stacy J. Rogers. 2009. *Alone Together: How Marriage in America Is Changing.* Cambridge, MA: Harvard University Press.

Baldwin, James. 1962. "As Much Truth as One Can Bear." *New York Times Book Review*, January 14.

Berger, Peter L., and Thomas Luckmann. 1991. *The Social Construction of Reality: A Treatise in the Sociology of Knowledge.* New York: Penguin.

Bradshaw, John. 1992. *Creating Love: The Next Great Stage of Growth.* New York: Bantam.

Centers for Disease Control and Prevention (CDC). 2024. "About Adverse Childhood Experiences (ACEs)." October 8. www.cdc.gov/violenceprevention/aces/index.html.

Centre for Addiction and Mental Health. n.d. "Trauma." Accessed March 29, 2025. www.camh.ca/en/health-info/mental-illness-and-addiction-index/trauma.

Cozolino, Louis. 2017. *The Neuroscience of Psychotherapy: Healing the Social Brain*, 3rd ed. New York: W. W. Norton.

Csikszentmihalyi, Mihaly. 1990. *Flow: The Psychology of Optimal Experience.* New York: Harper and Row.

Estés, Clarissa Pinkola. 1992. *Women Who Run with the Wolves: Myths and Stories of the Wild Woman Archetype.* New York: Ballantine.

Felitti, Vincent J., Robert F. Anda, Dale Nordenberg, et al. 1998. "Relationship of Childhood Abuse and Household Dysfunction to Many of the Leading Causes of Death in Adults: The Adverse Childhood Experiences (ACE) Study." *American Journal of Preventive Medicine* 14 (4): 245–258.

Fincham, Dylan S., Strauss C., Montero-Marín J., and Cavanagh K. 2023. "Breathing-Based Therapies for Anxiety and Depression: A Systematic Review." *Frontiers in Psychology* 14: 1182456. https://doi.org/10.3389/fpsyg.2023.1182456.

Fredrickson, Barbara L. 2001. "The Role of Positive Emotions in Positive Psychology." *American Psychologist* 56 (3): 218–226.

Fromm, Erich. 1956. *The Art of Loving*. New York: Harper and Brothers.

Graybiel, Ann M. 2008. "Habits, Rituals, and the Evaluative Brain." *Annual Review of Neuroscience* 31: 359–387. https://doi.org/10.1146/annurev.neuro.29.051605.112851.

Greene, Robert. 2012. *Mastery*. New York: Viking.

Griffiths, Roland R., William A. Richards, Matthew W. Johnson, Una D. McCann, and Robert Jesse. 2008. "Mystical-Type Experiences Occasioned by Psilocybin Mediate the Attribution of Personal Meaning and Spiritual Significance 14 Months Later." *Journal of Psychopharmacology* 22 (6): 621–632.

Hayes, Steven C., Jason B. Luoma, Frank W. Bond, Akihiko Masuda, and Jason Lillis. 2006. "Acceptance and Commitment Therapy: Model, Processes and Outcomes." *Behaviour Research and Therapy* 44 (1): 1–25. https://doi.org/10.1016/j.brat.2005.06.006.

hooks, bell. 2001. *All About Love: New Visions*. New York: Harper Perennial.

Kase, Taichi, Takayuki Ueno, Hiroki Shimoyama, and Kohei Oishi. 2021. "Gratitude and Mental Health: Systematic Review of Intervention Studies." *International Journal of Environmental Research and Public Health* 18 (24): 13071. https://doi.org/10.3390/ijerph182413071.

Lispector, Clarice. 2012. *Near to the Wild Heart*. Translated by Alison Entrekin. New York: New Directions.

McAdams, Tom A., Rosa Cheesman, and Yasmin I. Ahmadzadeh. 2022. "Annual Research Review. Towards a Deeper Understanding of Nature and Nurture: Combining Family-Based Quasi-Experimental Methods with Genomic Data." *Journal of Child Psychology and Psychiatry* 63 (4): 693–707.

Newberg, Andrew B., and Eugene G. d'Aquili. 2000. "The Neuropsychology of Religious and Spiritual Experience." *Journal of Consciousness Studies* 7 (11–12): 251–266.

Parthasarathy, A. 2014. *Vedanta Treatise: The Eternities*. Mumbai: Vedanta Life Institute.

Pascual-Leone, Antonio, and Leslie S. Greenberg. 2007. "Emotional Processing in Experiential Therapy: Why 'The Only Way Out Is Through.'" *Journal of Consulting and Clinical Psychology* 75 (6): 875–887.

Price, Neil S. 2011. "An Archaeology of Altered States: Shamanism and Material Culture." *Cambridge Archaeological Journal* 21 (3): 345–366. https://doi.org/10.1017/S0959774311000422.

Schwartz, Richard C. 2021. "Introduction." In *No Bad Parts: Healing Trauma and Restoring Wholeness with the Internal Family Systems Model*, 1–14. Boulder, CO: Sounds True.

Smith, John A., Emily R. Chen, and Luis M. Alvarez. 2023. "Infralimbic-Striatal Circuitry Enables Habit Disruption in Response to Novel Stimuli." *Nature Neuroscience* 26 (8): 1021–1030. https://doi.org/10.1038/s41593-023-01345-9.

Stone, Jay. 2005. "Carrey's Been Busted." *Ottawa Citizen*, December 16.

Substance Abuse and Mental Health Services Administration. n.d. "Child Trauma." Accessed March 29, 2025. www.samhsa.gov/mental-health/trauma-violence/child-trauma.

Tedeschi, Richard G., and Lawrence G. Calhoun. 2004. "Posttraumatic Growth: Conceptual Foundations and Empirical Evidence." *Psychological Inquiry* 15 (1): 1–18.

Teng, Lilian, Doris Leung, Amy Shum, and Amy H.Y. Ho. 2022. "Exploring the Role of Gratitude in Patients with Advanced Cancer Receiving Palliative Care: A Qualitative Study." *BMC Palliative Care* 21 (1): 206. https://doi.org/10.1186/s12904-022-01092-7.

Ulrich, Roger S. 1984. "View Through a Window May Influence Recovery from Surgery." *Science* 224 (4647): 420–421.

van der Kolk, Bessel. 2014. *The Body Keeps the Score: Brain, Mind, and Body in the Healing of Trauma*. New York: Viking.

van der Kolk, Bessel A., Laura Stone, Jennifer West, et al. 2014. "Yoga as an Adjunctive Treatment for Posttraumatic Stress Disorder: A Randomized Controlled Trial." *Journal of Clinical Psychiatry* 75 (6): e559–e565.

Wegner, Daniel M. 1994. "Ironic Processes of Mental Control." *Psychological Review* 101 (1): 34–52. https://doi.org/10.1037/0033-295X.101.1.34.

Yilmaz Balban, Melis, Elizabeth A. Feldman, Wendy Berry Mendes, David Spiegel, and Andrew D. Huberman. 2023. "Brief Structured Respiration Practices Enhance Mood and Reduce Physiological Arousal." *Cell Reports Medicine* 4, no. 1 (January 17): 100895. https://doi.org/10.1016/j.xcrm.2022.100895.

Zaccaro, Andrea, Andrea Piarulli, Marco Laurino, et al. 2018. "How Breath-Control Can Change Your Life: A Systematic Review on Psychophysiological Correlates of Slow Breathing." *Frontiers in Human Neuroscience* 12: 353. https://doi.org/10.3389/fnhum.2018.00353.

Zaccaro, Andrea, Erika Garbella, Alessandra Piarulli, and Angelo Gemignani. 2023. "Slow-Breathing Interventions for Stress Reduction: An Updated Meta-Analysis." *Frontiers in Psychology* 14 (2023): 1150079.

Index

About the Author

Millana Snow is a leading voice in global wellness and the founder of Integrative Breathwork, a modality that blends breath, energy healing, and personal inquiry to shift the subconscious mind. Since 2020, she has trained nearly two hundred facilitators in her method, expanding access to healing across the globe.

Millana's journey began with meditation at the age of four and has spanned decades of study in psychology, anthropology, and the world's spiritual traditions. Her mixed heritage and life across cultures inform a grounded, inclusive approach to healing that resonates with people from all walks of life. She has become a trusted guide for high-profile leaders, artists, and grassroots communities, supporting clients through deep transformation and reconnection to their inner power.

Millana has led immersive workshops and healing experiences around the world, including for Columbia University, New York University, Soho House, Popsugar Playground, the London Mind Body Spirit Festival, and more. As an artist, she co-led The Actor's Workshop with British actor and filmmaker DéObia Oparéi at Soho House in Los Angeles, where they explored the intersection of presence, embodiment, and creative expression.

She has taught Integrative Breathwork across the United States as well as in London, Barcelona, Berlin, and Japan, cultivating a global community of practitioners and clients. Her work has been featured in *Vogue*, *Harper's Bazaar*, *Marie Claire*, *Elle*, and dozens of other international outlets. She has appeared in campaigns for YSL, CoverGirl, Nike, Adidas, Disney, TOMS, and more. Millana is also a Webby Award winner for Best Travel + Adventure Show and was the winning model of *Project Runway*'s Season 8.

She lives in Northern California with her husband and their dog, Remy. This is her first book.

RAISING READERS

Books Build Bright Futures

Thank you for reading this book and for being a reader of books in general. We are so grateful to share being part of a community of readers with you, and we hope you will join us in passing our love of books on to the next generation of readers.

Did you know that reading for enjoyment is the single biggest predictor of a child's future happiness and success?

More than family circumstances, parents' educational background, or income, reading impacts a child's future academic performance, emotional well-being, communication skills, economic security, ambition, and happiness.

Studies show that kids reading for enjoyment in the US is in rapid decline:

- In 2012, 53% of 9-year-olds read almost every day. Just 10 years later, in 2022, the number had fallen to 39%.
- In 2012, 27% of 13-year-olds read for fun daily. By 2023, that number was just 14%.

Together, we can commit to **Raising Readers** and change this trend. How?

- Read to children in your life daily.
- Model reading as a fun activity.
- Reduce screen time.
- Start a family, school, or community book club.
- Visit bookstores and libraries regularly.
- Listen to audiobooks.
- Read the book before you see the movie.
- Encourage your child to read aloud to a pet or stuffed animal.
- Give books as gifts.
- Donate books to families and communities in need.

BOB1217

Books build bright futures, and **Raising Readers** is our shared responsibility.

For more information, visit **JoinRaisingReaders.com**

Sources: National Endowment for the Arts, National Assessment of Educational Progress, WorldBookDay.org, Nielsen BookData's 2023 "Understanding the Children's Book Consumer"